J.S. BACH

TWO-PART INVENTIONS

EDITED BY WILLARD A. PALMER

Facsimile of the Title Page of the Autograph of 1723

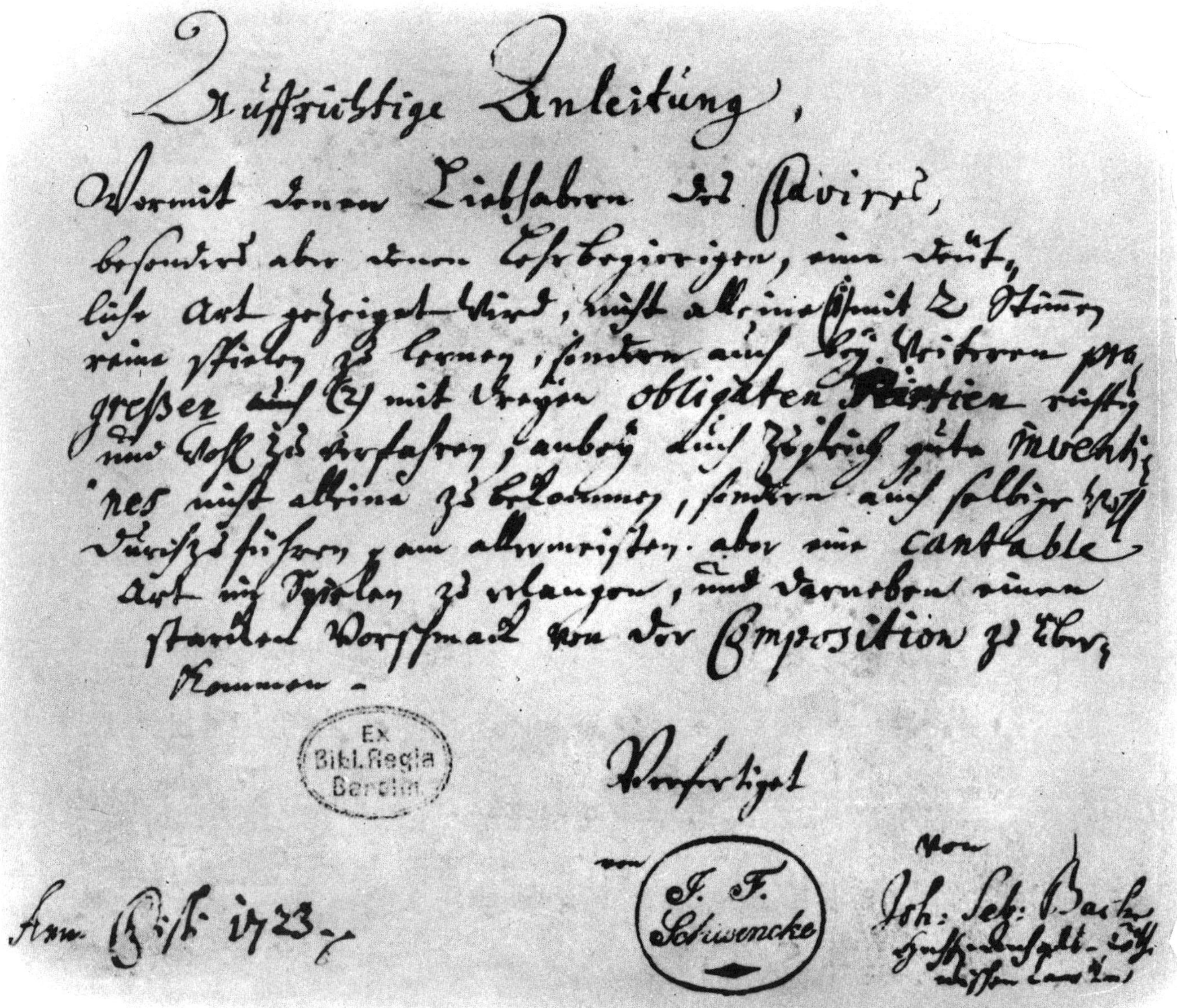

Sincere Instruction

in which lovers of keyboard music, and especially those desiring to learn to play, are shown a clear way not only (1) to learn to play cleanly in two parts, but also after further progress (2) to proceed correctly and well with three obbligato parts, and at the same time not only to compose good inventions, but to develop them well; but most of all to achieve a cantabile style in playing, and to acquire a taste for the elements of composition.

Prepared by
JOH. SEB. BACH,
Chapel Master to His Serene Highness,
the Prince of Anhalt-Cöthen.
The Year of our Lord: 1723

A General MIDI disk is available (5714) which includes a full piano recording.

Cover art: A portrait believed to be of Johann Sebastian Bach. ca. 1715
by Johann Ernst Rentsch. the elder
Museum der Stadt. Erfurt. Germany
Archiv für Kunst und Geschichte. Berlin. Germany

Sources used for This Edition

J. S. Bach's *Inventions* and *Sinfonias*, more commonly known as the *Two-Part Inventions* and *Three-Part Inventions*, were not published during Bach's lifetime. There are two authentic autographs:

1. The *Clavier-Büchlein vor Wilhelm Friedemann Bach*, which was begun in the year 1720, contains each of the 15 *Inventions* under the title *Preambulum*. The *Sinfonias* are contained in the same volume, each bearing the title *Fantasia*, but the *Sinfonia in C Minor* is missing and the *Sinfonia in D Major* is incomplete. Several of the *Inventions* are in the hand of Wilhelm Friedemann, but these certainly were written under the supervision of his father. Most of the *Inventions* and all of the *Sinfonias* are clearly in J. S. Bach's own hand. This manuscript is now in the library of the Yale School of Music at New Haven, Connecticut. A facsimile edition is published by Da Capo Press, New York.

2. The final and complete version, the *Autograph of 1723*, is entirely in J. S. Bach's own hand. This manuscript is in the possession of the Berlin State Library. A facsimile edition is published by Dover Publications, Inc., New York.

A number of interesting manuscript copies, made by pupils of Bach, or by members of the Bach family circle, are extant. Two of these, from the archives of the Berlin State Library, were found to he helpful in preparing this revised edition, particularly in checking Bach's original slurs and ornaments, which are not always perfectly clear in the autographs.

1. A manuscript formerly in the possession of Wilhelm Friedemann Bach. Bischoff believed it to be authentic, and referred to it in his edition as *"the second Autograph."* We will refer to this as *"the Friedemann manuscript."*

2. A manuscript in the hand of Heinrich Nikolaus Gerber, dated 1725. Gerber was Bach's pupil for several years, beginning in 1724.

Why Only 15 Inventions and Sinfonias?

The title page of Bach's autograph manuscript of the first volume of his *Well-Tempered Clavier* is dated 1722. This book contains 24 preludes and fugues; one in each major and minor key. Why, then, did Bach use only 15 keys in his *Inventions* and *Sinfonias*, the final autograph of which is dated 1723?

In composing the *Inventions* and *Sinfonias*, Bach chose to use the keys that could be acceptably applied to the old system of tuning in general use at the time. This system, which we now call *meantone* temperament, was known to the musicians of that day simply as "the method of tuning." It favored certain keys and made others impractical. Sharps could not function enharmonically as flats, or vice versa. In *meantone* temperament, as it was practiced in the 18th century and before, each key has its own special character, and the usable keys are more harmonious than the same keys are in *equal* temperament.

Meantone temperament is generally tuned to make the following tones function as harmoniously as possible when combined in various intervals:

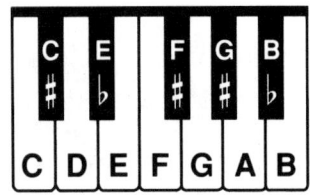

Thus, to make the *Inventions* and *Sinfonias* playable on instruments tuned according to the system in general use, Bach confined his selection of keys to those compatible with the *meantone* system. Actually, he very nearly went beyond the limits of the system by including the key of F minor. Since there was no true A-flat available (unless Bach used a *modified meantone* tuning, in which a few of the tones can sometimes be used enharmonically), the G-sharp key had to serve as an A-flat. The interval F to G-sharp (actually an augmented second) served as a very small minor third, making the character of the key considerably more "doleful" than the same key would have sounded in *equal* temperament. The key of F minor seems to have often been reserved for music of similar character.

The purpose of *The Well-Tempered Clavier*, on the other hand, was to introduce pieces in all major and minor keys. This was made possible through the use of a system of tuning known as *Well-temperament*, which not only made it possible to play in all keys, but also preserved, to a remarkable extent, the "characters of the keys." This system involves a compromise tuning that allows enharmonic relationships between sharps and flats, and slight adjustments that would allow, for example, an F-natural to serve as an E-sharp. One common misconception, found in some music textbooks, dictionaries and encyclopedias should be corrected: *Well-temperament* is definitely NOT the same as our presently used system of *equal* temperament, which divides the octave into 12 equally out-of-tune semitones. In this system, the "characters of the keys" are destroyed, the only difference in the sounds of the keys being a matter of highness or lowness in pitch.

For further study of the historical temperaments, two books by Owen Jorgensen are highly recommended: *Tuning the Historical Temperaments by Ear*, Northern Michigan University Press, Marquette, 1977, and *TUNING/Containing/The Perfection of Eighteenth Century Temperament/The Lost Art of Nineteenth Century Temperament/and/The Science of Equal Temperament*, Michigan State University Press, East Lansing, 1991. Articles contained in the latter volume convincingly prove that true *equal* temperament was not practiced on pianos before 1885, and was not commonly practiced on pianos before the 20th century.

THE IMPORTANCE OF THE CLAVIER-BÜCHLEIN

The *Clavier-Büchlein* is actually a music instruction book, devised by J. S. Bach for his eldest son, Wilhelm Friedemann, and probably also used by his younger children, including Carl Philipp Emanuel and Johann Christian. The first versions of the *Inventions* and *Sinfonias* are believed to have been composed at Wilhelm Friedemann's lessons. Since, in the foreword to the *Autograph of 1723* (see page 1) J. S. Bach stated that the purpose of these pieces included "how to compose good inventions and develop them well ... and to acquire a taste for the elements of composition," it is important to know as much as possible about how Bach presented these works to Wilhelm Friedemann.

The order of the *Inventions*, and also the *Sinfonias*, as they appear in the *Autograph of 1723*, is as follows:

C, Cm, D, Dm, E-flat, E, Em, F, Fm, G, Gm, A, Am, B-flat, Bm.

The present edition places them in the above order, as do all modern editions.

In the *Clavier-Büchlein*, however, Bach presented them to his son in the order of the ascending diatonic scale, from C major to B minor, with the remaining pieces in descending order, from B-flat major down to C minor, as follows:

C, Dm, Em, F, G, Am, Bm, B-flat, A, Gm, Fm, E, E-flat, D, Cm.

The first three *Two-Part Inventions* (C major, D minor and E minor) are based on scales or portions of scales; the next three (F major, G major and A minor) are derived from broken chords. The next (B minor) uses a combination of both ideas, but emphasizes contrapuntal development, and is, essentially, a two-voice fugue. The pieces that follow, in descending order of keys, continue to show that Bach was a well-organized teacher. Modern teachers will no doubt agree that this is a logical order for presenting these pieces to students, particularly when emphasis is placed on teaching the various devices used in their composition.

It is possible that Wilhelm Friedemann himself may have composed, or at least participated in the composition of some of these pieces, supervised by his father. In the *Clavier-Büchlein*, the C major and D minor *Two-Part Inventions* are in Wilhelm Friedemann's hand, with a few emendations by his father. The E minor, F major, G major, A minor and B minor *Two-Part Inventions* are entirely in Wilhelm Friedemann's hand. After the completion of the ascending series, the father's hand definitely takes over for the remaining eight pieces in the descending series.

In the *Autograph of 1723*, all of the *Inventions* and *Sinfonias* are in the hand of J. S. Bach.

The Explication

The following table of ornaments, from the *Clavier-Büchlein*, entitled "Explication unterschiedlicher Zeichen, so gewisse Manieren artig zu spielen, andeuten" is the only such table ever prepared by J. S. Bach.

The above table is reproduced below in modern notation.

Explanation of various signs, showing how to play certain ornaments properly.

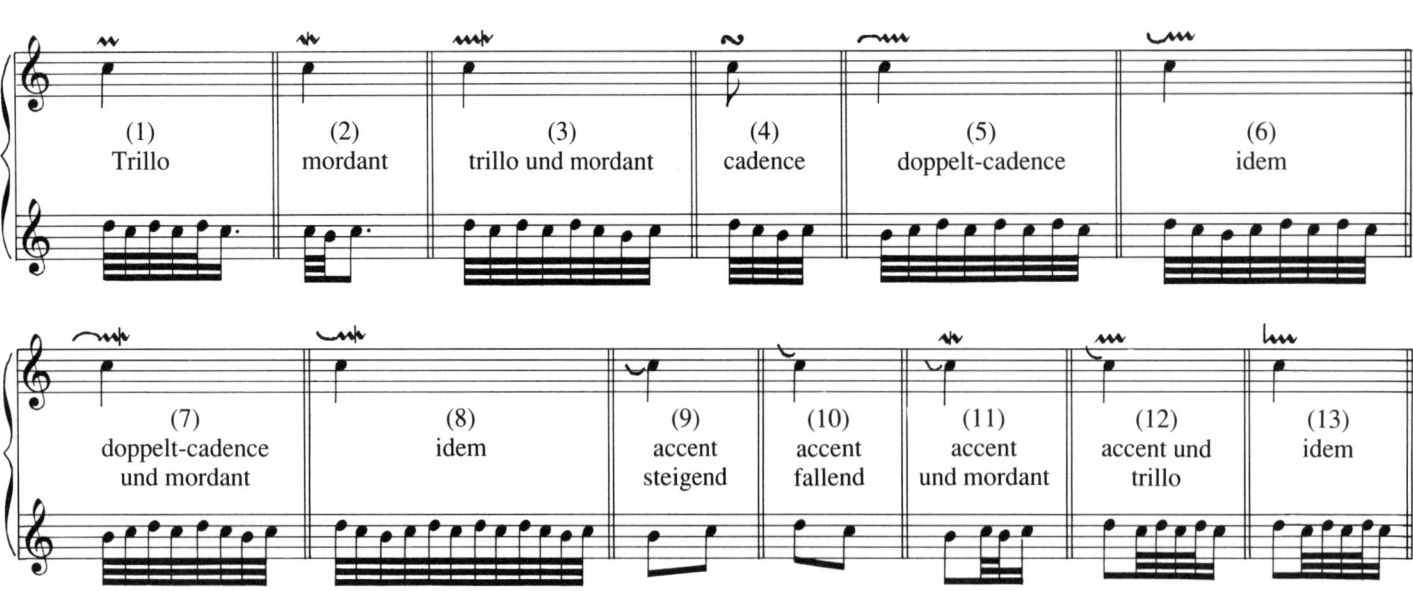

The most common English names of the above ornaments are:

(1) Trill   (2) Mordent   (3) Trill with termination   (4) Turn   (5) Ascending trill   (6) Descending trill

(7) Ascending trill with termination   (8) Descending trill with termination   (9) Appoggiatura from below   (10) Appoggiatura from above   (11) Appoggiatura and mordent   (12) Appoggiatura and trill   (13) The same

Because the *Clavier-Büchlein* was in private ownership until 1932, when it was purchased by the library of the Yale School of Music, it was not easily available for use in editions prepared before that year. This includes the *Bach-Gesellschaft, Busoni, Czerny* and *Mason* editions. Hans Bischoff had access to it only after he had completed his edition of the *Inventions* and *Sinfonias* and made a few incomplete references to it in a supplementary table, overlooking a great deal of important information. While the *Autograph of 1723* must be considered the final revision, and consequently the version most approved by J. S. Bach, the value of the *Clavier-Büchlein* in establishing an authentic and accurate text is easily illustrated by the following examples:

In *Invention No. 3*, one of the ornaments has caused considerable confusion. It appears in the third measure and again in the 45th measure, which is identical. In the *Autograph of 1723* this ornament has the appearance of ∿, but it appears over a 16th note! The ornament bears little resemblance to Bach's manner of writing the "doppelt cadence und mordant" (see the *Explication* from the *Clavier-Büchlein* on page 4 of this edition). It is clearly impossible to execute at any reasonable tempo, since it involves playing eight notes in the time occupied by a 16th note. In spite of the fact that it is unplayable, it is found in the *Bach-Gesellschaft* edition without comment. Hans Bischoff refers to it as the authentic ornament but assigns it to a footnote, thus indicating his concern.

When these measures from the final autograph are compared with the corresponding measures in the *Clavier-Büchlein*, the problem disappears:

Facsimile from the *Autograph of 1723*

3rd measure: 45th measure:

   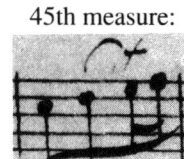

Facsimile from the *Clavier-Büchlein*

3rd measure: 45th measure:

The ornament is NOT ∿, as it appears in some editions. It is very clearly a slur followed by a mordent: ⌒ ∿

The above examples and the upper staffs of the manuscript below are written in the *soprano clef*, which places middle C on the lowest line of the staff.

In the 1723 autograph of *Sinfonia (Three-Part Invention) No. 11*, in measure 50, an ink blot just above an e-flat has caused all other editors to misinterpret the note as an f.

Autograph of 1723:

e-flat or f?

Bach-Gesellschaft edition (the same notes are found in the *Henle, Bärenreiter, Peters, Wiener Urtext, Kalmus* and *Schirmer* editions):

f

Clavier-Büchlein (1720):

e-flat

Gerber manuscript (1725):

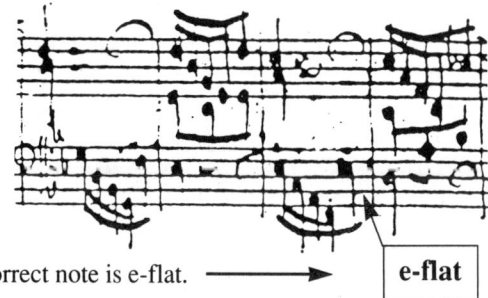

e-flat

⟵ The correct note is e-flat. ⟶

In order to make the pitch of the notes referred to in our text and in the footnotes perfectly clear, we have chosen to use a modified version of the Helmholtz pitch notation.

Helmholtz used C-B, c-b, c'-b', c''-b'', c'''-b'''. We use C-B, c-b, c^1-b^1, c^2-b^2, c^3-b^3, as follows:

C-B =    c-b =  c^1-b^1 =  c^2-b^2 =  c^3-b^3 =

THE USE OF ORNAMENTS IN THE INVENTIONS AND SINFONIAS

Since the *Explication* applies each ornament to a quarter note only, and that application is only practical at a moderate tempo, it can only show the *GENERAL CONFIGURATION* of each ornament. Note that all ornaments in the table begin *on the beat*. They are played diatonically in the keys in force at the moment they occur, with very few exceptions.

1. THE TRILL

These symbols are used interchangeably to indicate a long or short trill.

All trills begin on the *upper note*.

The trill may be rather freely interpreted by the performer. It may come to rest on the principal note or, at times, continue for the entire value of the note. The minimum number of notes in any trill is four.

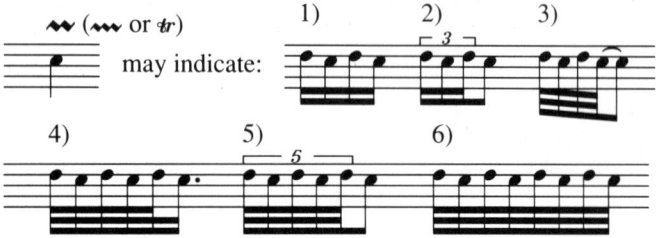

A trill is sometimes made more effective by lingering slightly on the first note.

Trills on longer notes may consume the entire value of the note or may stop on any beat or fraction of a beat.

Some artists and teachers insist on playing the first trill in *Invention No. 1* as a mordent. This error has its origin in old editions of *Czerny* and *Busoni*. In the *Autograph of 1723* as well as in the *Clavier-Büchlein*, the ornament is clearly a trill, indicated by the symbol ᮰. The *Gerber manuscript* also has a trill, indicated by the symbol *tr*.

2. THE MORDENT

The word "mordent" is derived from the Latin *mordere*, meaning "to bite." This suggests that mordents should have an incisive quality. They contribute brilliance and sometimes serve to accentuate the rhythm. They should generally be played quite rapidly; sometimes even more quickly than these realizations show:

In extremely rapid passages, it is effective to strike both notes simultaneously, then immediately release the lower note (C. P. E. Bach, *ESSAY,* * II, v, 3).

Sometimes, on long notes, a mordent may have additional repercussions. It is then called a *LONG MORDENT*. Sometimes this is done when the ordinary mordent sign is used, but often this is indicated by the sign ᮰ or ᮰. The function of the long mordent is different from that of the normal or short mordent. It fills out the value of the note.

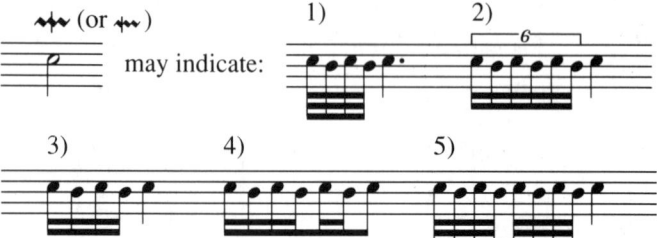

When a mordent is used to fill out a note, it cannot consume the entire value of the note. "A small portion of its original value must be left plain, since even the best used mordent sounds terrible when carried, like a trill, directly into the following note" (C. P. E. Bach, *ESSAY*, II, v, 8). In the same work, in II, v, 11, we read, "the brilliance of a mordent is often enhanced by raising its lower note one half step." Thus a mordent is not inevitably played diatonically.

3. THE TRILL WITH TERMINATION

This is sometimes called the *TRILL WITH SUFFIX*, or the *TRILL WITH TURNED ENDING*, or, less often, the *TRILL AND MORDENT*.

The *termination* consists of two closing notes, connected to the trill and generally played at the same speed as the trill repercussions.

The trill itself requires a minimum of four notes, and the termination requires two additional notes; thus the minimum number of notes in the entire ornament is six:

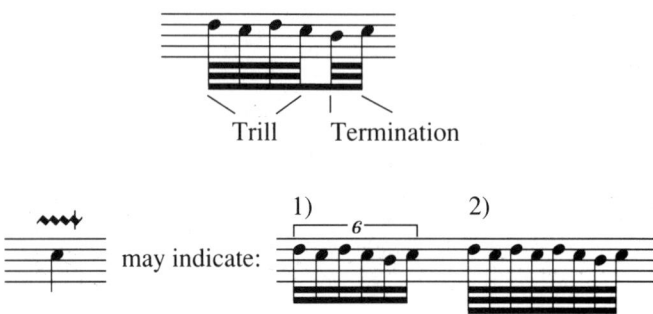

*C. P. E. Bach, *Versuch über die wahre Art das Clavier zu spielen* (Essay on the True Art of Keyboard Playing). Berlin, 1753.

The termination is often written out in full, as in the second measure of *Invention No. 2*. In such a case the trill is played at the same speed as the closing notes.

Invention No. 2
(2nd measure)

written: played:

In his *ESSAY*, II, iii, 13, C. P. E. Bach comments that a trill may have an added termination when there is time, whether it is indicated or not. These are better when the trilled note ascends to the following note but may be added regardless of stepwise ascent or descent.

Bach indicated terminations on the long trills in *Invention No. 12*, but did not in *Invention No. 4*.

4. THE TURN ∾

In his manuscripts, J. S. Bach used a vertical or sloping sign for the turn: ⌇

The turn in Bach's music always begins on the note *above* the principal note.

In his *ESSAY*, II, iv, 3, C. P. E. Bach says, "The turn is almost always performed rapidly." He gives the following examples, in which the manner of performance of the turn is shown to depend upon the tempo of the music:

According to the section of C. P. E. Bach's *ESSAY* just cited, the turn is a miniature suffixed trill, in effect, and can be used as a simplification of same.

When the turn is placed *between* two notes, it is played after the principal note has been sounded. The rhythm of the turn must then be determined by the amount of time available for it. There are usually several acceptable solutions:

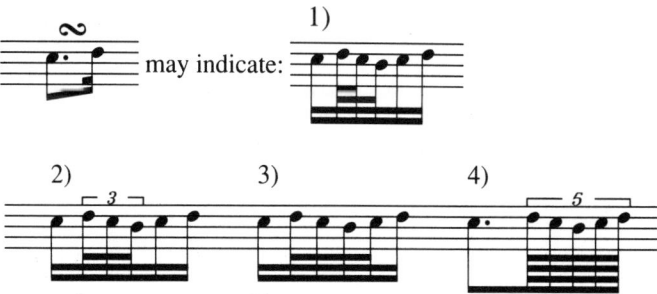

For an example of such a turn, see *Invention No. 9*, measure 16.

5. THE TRILL WITH PREFIX FROM BELOW ⌒᷉

This is sometimes called the *ASCENDING TRILL*. The prefix consists of two notes; the trill requires at least four notes; thus the minimum number of notes for the entire ornament is six.

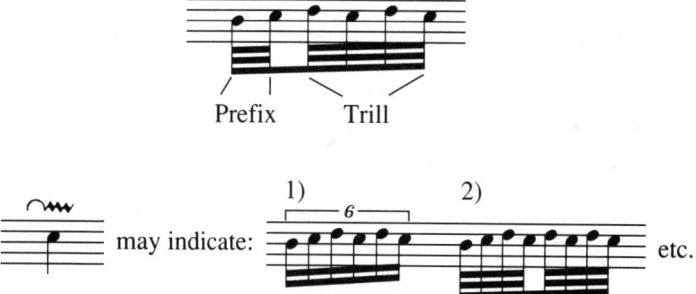

Since this ornament is usually employed on long notes, and since long trills are usually best played with a termination, this ornament, in practice, usually becomes a *TRILL WITH PREFIX FROM BELOW, WITH TERMINATION* (see No. 7, below). In the *Inventions* and *Sinfonias*, the only example of its use without a termination is in the 16th measure of *Invention No. 9:*

Invention No. 9
(16th measure)

written: played:

6. THE TRILL WITH PREFIX FROM ABOVE ᷉᷉

This is sometimes called the *DESCENDING TRILL*. The prefix from above consists of four notes, and is similar to the turn. The trill requires at least four notes; thus the minimum number of notes for the entire ornament is eight.

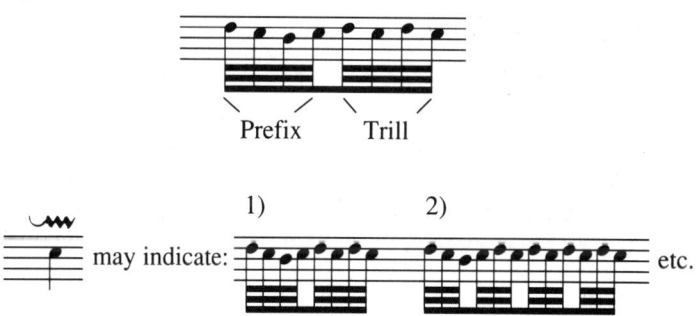

In practice this ornament is usually replaced with a *TRILL WITH PREFIX FROM ABOVE, WITH TERMINATION* (see No. 8, below). The repercussions need not be measured.

7. THE TRILL WITH PREFIX FROM BELOW, WITH TERMINATION ⌒⋀⋀↓

This is sometimes called the *ASCENDING TRILL, WITH TERMINATION* (or *SUFFIX*).

This ornament consists of three parts: the prefix, the trill, and the suffix (termination). It cannot be played with fewer than eight notes, as shown in the *Explication:*

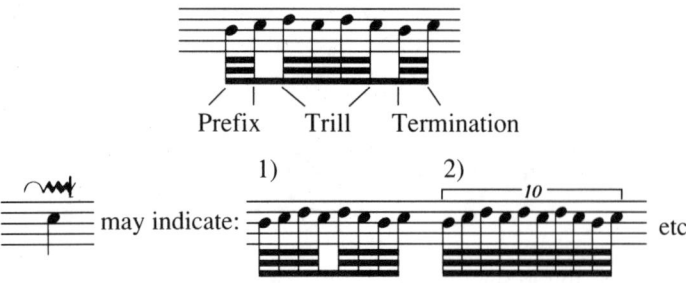

Prefix   Trill   Termination

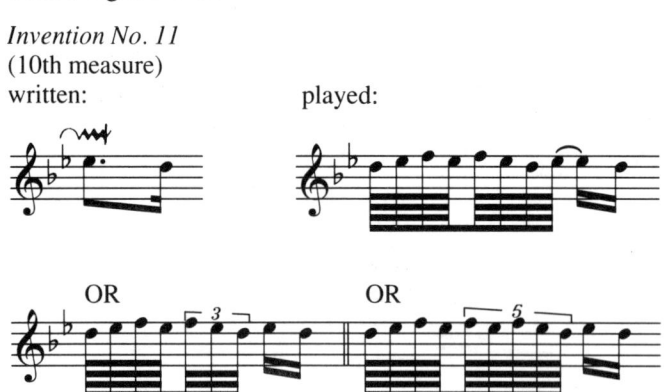

The termination is sometimes written out in full. It may also be added to a trill with a prefix when followed by a stepwise ascent.

This ornament is usually executed only on notes of considerable length, but it appears in *Invention No. 11* over a dotted eighth note.

Invention No. 11
(10th measure)
written: played:

The ornament is used several times in *Invention No. 12:*

Invention No. 12
(1st measure)
written:

played:

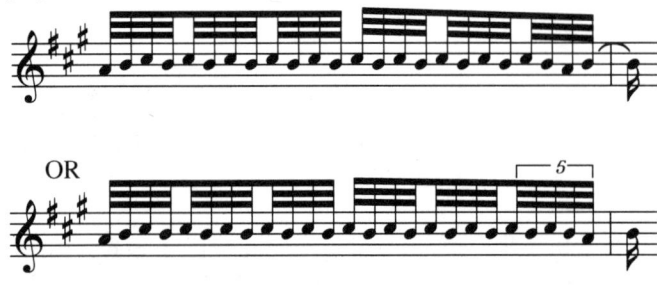

A trill of this length does not require an exact number of repercussions. Like the normal trill, it may begin slowly and accelerate as it proceeds.

8. THE TRILL WITH PREFIX FROM ABOVE, WITH TERMINATION ⌒⋀⋀↓

This is sometimes called the *DESCENDING TRILL, WITH TERMINATION* (or *SUFFIX*).

This ornament requires at least two notes more than the one previously discussed, thus it usually occurs only on long notes.

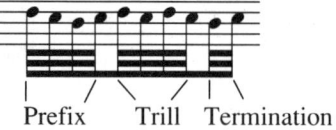

Prefix   Trill   Termination

Because the last two notes of the trill combine with the termination to produce a sound exactly like the prefix, it is best to include several additional repercussions of the trill whenever the length of the note permits. The *Explication* makes this clear:

This ornament is most frequently used on long notes, but it appears in *Invention No. 5* over a quarter note:

Invention No. 5
(32nd measure)
written:

played:

NOTE:
Compound ornaments 5 through 8 begin with prefixes. The curved shape of the beginning of the sign for each of these ornaments is a graphic indication of the contour of the first four notes of each ornament. The remaining portion of each sign shows how the rest of the ornament is played (either as a trill, or a trill with a mordent ending). With this in mind, the interpretation of each of these ornaments is very simple to understand and easy to remember:

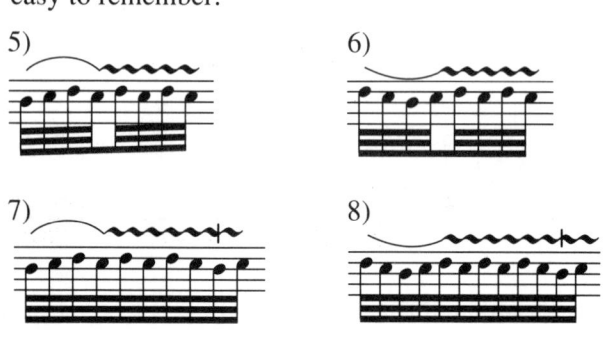

9–12. THE APPOGGIATURA INDICATED BY ORNAMENT ONLY ⌐ ◡

The small hook may have been derived from the slur that is used with a small note indicating an appoggiatura.

The word "appoggiatura" is derived from the Italian *appoggiare*, meaning "to lean."

If the hook comes from below the main note, a *LOWER* or *ASCENDING APPOGGIATURA* is used. The note a diatonic step or half step below the principal note is played on the beat of the principal note. This note receives the accent and resolves more softly to the main note. If the hook comes from above the main note, the *UPPER* or *DESCENDING APPOGGIATURA* is used. When the value of the main note is divisible by two, the appoggiatura is given half of that value:

9. *Ascending Appoggiatura*   10. *Descending Appoggiatura*

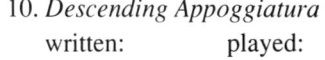

An appoggiatura used with a dotted note usually receives two-thirds of the value of the principal note:

written: played: written: played:

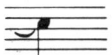   

Examples 11 and 12 in the *Explication* show the appoggiatura used with the mordent or the trill. Note that in example 12, the appoggiatura becomes the starting note of the trill. (See also 13, *THE PREPARED TRILL*, which is just another way of indicating the same ornament as that shown in example 12.)

11. *Appoggiatura and Mordent* 12. *Appoggiatura and Trill*

written: played: written: played:

Note that in both of the above examples, the appoggiatura portion of the ornament is given its usual value, in this case, half the value of the principal note.

THE APPOGGIATURA INDICATED BY SMALL NOTES ♪♩♪♫

Most of the appoggiaturas in *The Well-Tempered Clavier* are written in small notes.

In playing these appoggiaturas, the same rules are observed as those outlined for the hook. All appoggiaturas are played on the beat and receive the accent.

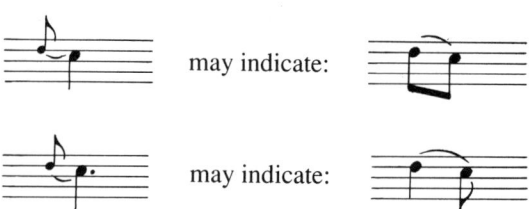

may indicate:

may indicate:

> **IMPORTANT!**
> The modern acciaccatura or "grace note" ♪ appears in many modern editions of the music of J. S. Bach. It was *never* used by Bach and it is *always* incorrect!

Of the relatively few appoggiaturas that appear in the *Inventions* and *Sinfonias*, those occurring before dotted notes are the ones most subject to varying interpretations. In the last measure of *Invention No. 5* some artists prefer to give the appoggiatura less than two-thirds of the value of the dotted note:

Invention No. 5
(last measure)
written:

played:

In this case, the total time value of the large notes is incomplete by one 32nd note. It would seem that Bach intended for the appoggiatura to be played as an eighth note. The principal note would then fit in as the missing 32nd note. For this reason, the first example seems to be the best solution. However, the second example is acceptable and frequently used.

In the ornamented version of *Sinfonia No. 5* there are many appoggiaturas before eighth notes and before dotted eighth notes. Those before eighth notes receive half the value of the note. Most performers give the appoggiaturas before the dotted notes only one-third of the value of the notes, or even less, possibly to keep the principal note from losing its identity. The performer may prefer to play them according to the rules of the period, giving them two-thirds of the value of the dotted note.

Sinfonia No. 5
(3rd measure)
written:

played:

THE APPOGGIATURA USED AS A PASSING TONE

When a passage descending by thirds contains appoggiatura signs (hooks or small notes), the appoggiaturas may (at the discretion of the performer) be used to fill in the interval of the third and are played very quickly.

The following examples are identical in meaning:

The notes may be played in rhythms appropriate to the character of the selection:

When used in this fashion, the small notes do not function as appoggiaturas, but simply as *passing tones*.

Invention No. 3 contains examples that may be considered important evidence that Bach, at least occasionally, used the small note or the hook to indicate a passing tone.

In the *Autograph of 1723*, these measures appear as follows:

4th measure: 46th measure:

In the *Clavier-Büchlein*, the same measures appear as follows:

4th measure: 46th measure:

   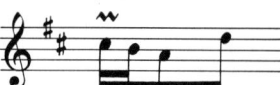

While it is true that measure 46 is not identical to the fourth measure, it seems clear that Bach wanted the passing appoggiatura in the 46th measure because he writes it out in full in the *Clavier-Büchlein*. Thus we may assume that he wanted it played the same in the fourth measure.

In this editor's opinion, this is the ONLY context in which appoggiaturas may be played ahead of the beat in the music of J. S. Bach. The *ON-THE-BEAT APPOGGIATURA* is possibly the *MOST EXPRESSIVE* of all ornaments, and it is usually advisable to use them even between descending thirds!

13. THE PREPARED TRILL

J. S. Bach used the same name for this ornament as for 12, the *APPOGGIATURA AND TRILL*. The appoggiatura is treated as a prolongation of the starting note of the trill.

written: played:

A prepared trill appears in *Invention No. 9*, in the 15th measure.

Invention No. 9
(15th measure)

written:

played:

The 13 ornaments contained in Bach's table have been discussed. Three additional ornaments remain to be explained.

---

14. THE SCHLEIFER

This ornament may also be called the "slide." The zig-zag portion of the ornament has nothing to do with a trill or mordent, but serves to mark the line or space upon which the ornament begins. When this sign is used, the two lower neighboring diatonic notes are played on the beat of the principal note and quickly slurred to the principal note.

    may indicate:

The schleifer does not appear in either of the two autograph manuscripts of the *Inventions* and *Sinfonias*, but it is used several times in the *Friedemann manuscript*.

Examples of the realization of the schleifer will be found in the footnotes of *Sinfonias No. 4, 7, 9* and *13*.

15. THE PRALLTRILLER

The pralltriller ("compact trill") is not included in the *Explication*, but it is discussed at length by C. P. E. Bach in his *ESSAY*, II, iii, 30–32.

The pralltriller may occur only after a descending second. The note that is ornamented with the trill must be preceded by the note one diatonic step higher. The pralltriller is played like an extremely rapid trill. It contains only four notes, the first of which is tied to the preceding note.

C. P. E. Bach says that it "joins the preceding note to the decorated one, and therefore never appears over detached notes." In every example in his *ESSAY*, he joins the two notes with a slur:

written: played:

We must emphasize that a pralltriller is not merely a normal trill tied to the preceding upper second. C. P. E. Bach says, "the pralltriller … is distinguished from the others by its speed and brevity." He also says, "Unlike other embellishments, it cannot be demonstrated slowly to students. It must literally crackle. It must be snapped on its final appearance … with such exceeding speed that the individual tones are heard with difficulty. Because of this, its acuteness stands beyond comparison with other trills."

If a pralltriller is employed in the first measure of *Invention No. 1*, it cannot be played any slower than the example shown below:

Invention No. 1
(1st measure)
written:

played (if pralltriller is used):

Because of the absence of a slur from the previous note, we believe that this ornament should be played as a normal short trill:

16. THE SCHNELLER

This ornament is translated as "the snap." It is not a substitute for the short trill, although it has been used in this fashion by many editors of Bach's keyboard works, including Busoni, Mason and several modern editors. Some editors write this ornament as the realization of a short trill, and then compound their error by calling it a pralltriller. In his *ESSAY*, II, viii, 1–4, C. P. E. Bach says that the notes of the schneller are always written out in the style of two-note appoggiaturas (but without a slur) and that it is always played rapidly:

written: played:

Those editors who use the schneller as a substitute for a trill (when the trill is preceded by the note one diatonic step higher) for the purpose of "preserving a legato" should consider that C. P. E. Bach also said that it "appears only before quick, detached notes." The tendency to use this ornament as a substitute for a short trill is evidence that there are still those among us who think that ∿ is an inverted mordent. C. P. E. Bach does not even mention the schneller as part of his discussion of the trill but takes it up as a separate subject. The schneller is not mentioned in the *Explication*, and there is no evidence that it should be used in any of the *Inventions* and *Sinfonias*.

17. ARPEGGIATION OF CHORDS

The practice of arpeggiating or "breaking" chords was so generally employed on the harpsichord and clavichord during Bach's day that it was not considered necessary to notate it in the music. When arpeggiation is indicated, the chord may be even more broadly spread. No chord sounds very good on the harpsichord without at least some slight degree of spreading.

Chords may be broken beginning with the top note or the lower note. If there is enough time, they may be broken in both directions, particularly in chords near the end of the piece (especially in preludes that have an improvisatory character).

Invention No. 1 ends with a closing chord, with an arpeggio sign indicated by the composer. *Invention No. 8* also ends with a closing chord, but with no arpeggiation indicated. It may be arpeggiated, however, at the discretion of the performer.

MORE ABOUT THE UPPER-NOTE TRILL

In his *ESSAY*, II, iii, 1–5, C. P. E. Bach outlines eight contexts in which trills may be used: 1) on the repetition of a note, 2) in stepwise passages, 3) in leaping passages, 4) in succession, 5) in cadences, 6) on sustained notes, 7) at fermatas, and 8) at caesuras. After listing these uses, he adds, "The trill always begins on the tone above the principal note."

Can C. P. E. Bach's principles be applied to J. S. Bach's music? In no case does C. P. E. Bach's discussion of any ornament disagree with his father's table. His discussion of their application agrees with the ways his father applies them. An example is the *APPLICATIO* and other pieces he wrote for another son, Wilhelm Friedemann, in the *Clavier-Büchlein*. The son's book can serve as a companion to the father's, and by studying the two together we become more enlightened. We see that the things J. S. Bach taught one son were taught identically to the other. C. P. E. Bach wrote, "My father was my only teacher, and everything I know, I learned from him."

Proper baroque performance practices, along with the correct execution of baroque ornaments, have been rediscovered in the 20th century, beginning with the brilliant pioneering efforts of Arnold Dolmetsch, who revealed his findings in his still excellent book, *THE INTERPRETATION OF THE MUSIC OF THE XVII & XVIII CENTURIES, REVEALED BY CONTEMPORARY EVIDENCE* (London, 1915). Scholars such as Howard Ferguson, Thurston Dart, Michael Collins, Putnam Aldrich, David Fuller, and a host of others, have added important evidence in theses and various articles published in the scholarly journals. Arnold Dolmetsch's work has been diligently carried on by his son, Carl Dolmetsch, and by his brilliant student, Robert Donington, in his valuable book, *THE INTERPRETATION OF EARLY MUSIC* (London, 1963; newly revised and enlarged version, New York, 1973). Also important is the same author's *A PERFORMER'S GUIDE TO BAROQUE MUSIC* (New York, 1973). Through the objective studies of these and other scholars, the trill from the upper auxiliary has been firmly established as standard baroque performance practice.

In view of the knowledge we now possess, including 17th- and 18th-century table after table showing all simple trills beginning on the beat and on the upper note, and all prefixed trills beginning on the beat, it is amazing and annoying that we still so frequently encounter trills beginning on the main note and/or ahead of the beat, not only in recordings of famous artists, but also in lectures and articles by musicians who should know better.

In Alfred Kreutz's *BEMERKUNGEN ZUM VORTRAG* (Observations about Execution) published with his edition of *The Well-Tempered Clavier*, Vol. I, by C. F. Peters, he recommends that about two-thirds of the trills should begin on the main note. The reason is simply that Kreutz believes, as too many others do, that a trill preceded by an upper second must begin on the main note, to avoid repeating the preceding note! This is in disagreement with all the examples we have from C. P. E. Bach, Couperin, D'Angelbert, Marpurg, Agricola, Türk, Quantz and many, many others. Not one of Bach's contemporaries has mentioned such a rule. In C. P. E. Bach's *ESSAY*, II, iii, 16, there are many examples of trills on notes preceded by upper seconds. C. P. E. Bach also points out that "trills are often used on a descending second, precisely where a mordent would be unsuitable."

F. W. Marpurg, in his *ANLEITUNG*,* I, iv, 7, wrote, "A trill, wherever it may stand, begins with the accessory note. If the upper note, with which the trill should begin, immediately precedes the trilled note, that note must be repeated with a new attack; or, before one begins the trill, it must be connected by means of a tie to the preceding note."

The upper-note trill functions melodically, harmonically, and expressively like an upper appoggiatura. Just as an upper appoggiatura is most effective when it repeats the preceding note, so is the trill most effective in the same context. In fact, the most important use of a trill is in cadences such as the following one:

The note preceding the trilled note serves as preparation for a suspension. This same note is repeated and reiterated as the upper note of the trill, and this produces the effect of suspension. The resolution occurs when the trill ends on the main note:

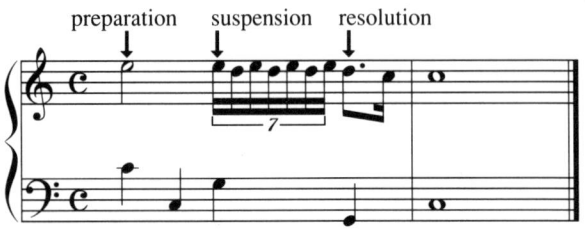

The lengthening of the value of the dot and shortening of the following note is explained in a subsequent section. The effectiveness of this upper-note trill may be tested by playing the same passage, beginning the trill on the principal note. The expressiveness produced by the dissonant sound of the upper note disappears. The dissonance-resolution effect is one of the most expressive sounds in music, and it represents an important function of the trill in many of its contexts.

Even in those passages where beginning the trill on the upper note does not produce such an effect, the present editor is convinced, just as Robert Donington says he is (*INTERPRETATION OF EARLY MUSIC*, pages

---

* Friedrich Wilhelm Marpurg, *Anleitung zum Klavierspielen* (Introduction to Keyboard Playing), Berlin, 1755.

632–633), that the trill was begun habitually on the upper note during this period, even when it was not particularly functional, from a harmonic standpoint, to do so.

Even as late as 1789, Daniel Gottlob Türk, in his *KLAVIERSCHULE* (Leipzig & Halle), III, 33, labels all main-note trills "incorrect." His illustrations show upper-note trills which reiterate the preceding upper seconds, even in chains of descending seconds. He also shows that even trills in the bass begin on the upper auxiliary.

Frederick Neumann, in his book, *ORNAMENTATION IN BAROQUE AND POST- BAROQUE MUSIC*, Princeton, New Jersey, 1978, shows a number of instances in which he believes certain trills in the music of J. S. Bach might best be begun on the principal note. This is an important reference work, and its contents should be viewed with respect by every serious student of Bach's music. In doing so, however, it is recommended that Robert Donington's discussion of Neumann's beliefs, on pages 620–640 of his above-mentioned book, be carefully studied and considered.

THE EXTEMPORIZATION OF ORNAMENTS

We may safely say that any musician of J. S. Bach's time who played the *Inventions* and *Sinfonias* using only the ornaments indicated would have been regarded as a very unimaginative performer. The practice of adding ornaments to the text has been frowned upon in recent years, but there are no grounds for this attitude, and it may even result in a performance lacking in style and authenticity.

There are two particularly important situations that may require addition of ornaments to the text. In these cases, the ornaments have often been omitted from the manuscripts because it was obvious that they should be there and a written ornament seemed unnecessary, and perhaps even insulting, to any player who was familiar with the general practices of the period.

The most important of these situations occurs when a cadential formula such as 𝅘𝅥𝅭 𝅘𝅥𝅮 | 𝅗𝅥 is used. (See the example in the previous section.) A trill on the first note is obligatory, whether indicated or not.

The other occasion often calling for the addition of ornaments is in the recurrence of thematic material that has been ornamented on its first appearance. In fact, when any recurrent theme is ornamented in any of its entries, one might consider using the same ornaments at all the appearances of the theme. One of J. S. Bach's students, E. L. Gerber, made the statement (*LEXICON*, 1790) that Bach played the ornaments in the themes of his works even when they occurred in the pedal part of an organ selection. C. P. E. Bach remarks that "all imitations should be exact in every detail."

When the ornament is one of the most important characteristics of a particular theme, there is little doubt that it should be played each time the theme occurs, if possible.

In some of the *Inventions* and *Sinfonias* it may be observed that J. S. Bach ornamented the right-hand entries, but not the left-hand ones. In these cases the player must judge whether the "missing" ornaments are to be added.

In addition to the situations mentioned above, in which the addition of certain unwritten ornaments is more or less obligatory, it should be noted that the practice of adding ornaments *ex tempore* was a part of "the manner of playing" learned by every student of music during Bach's day. Each performer was expected to heighten the expression or the *Affekt* (emotional content) of the music by the judicious addition of appropriate embellishments. Audiences of that day, schooled in understanding the performance practices of the period, applauded the tasteful addition of embellishments that made the performance more brilliant or more expressive, as the contexts demanded.

Invention No. 7, for example, provides many situations in which ornaments may be effectively added. Mordents are most effective on upward steps or leaps, and in the bass, on a note just before the downward leap of an octave (just as, in this case, the piece begins). A schleifer is effective in the treble voice on an upward leap, particularly on a leap of a fourth, and would work well on the fourth count of measure 10.

Trills work well on notes that descend from the previous upper second. Bach himself indicates a trill in this precise context on the first beat of the second measure, and again on the fourth beat of the same measure. It is profitable to notice how often Bach ascends by step or leap to a mordent, and how often he descends by step to a trill in the ornaments he has indicated in this composition.

Passing tones may often be effectively added between skips of a third.

Much may be learned by listening to performances by artists who are skilled in the art of adding ornaments to baroque keyboard music. Among the best of these are harpsichordist Igor Kipnis and pianist Andras Schiff.

DOTTED RHYTHMS IN THE BAROQUE PERIOD

In the Baroque period, the value of a dot after a note was not always strictly observed. In his *ESSAY*, III, i, 23, C. P. E. Bach states, "Short notes which follow dotted notes are always shorter in execution than their notation indicates." He also said, "Short notes which precede dotted ones are also played more rapidly than their notation indicates." He suggests adding another beam to the short notes, which would mean that the value of the dot should be lengthened.

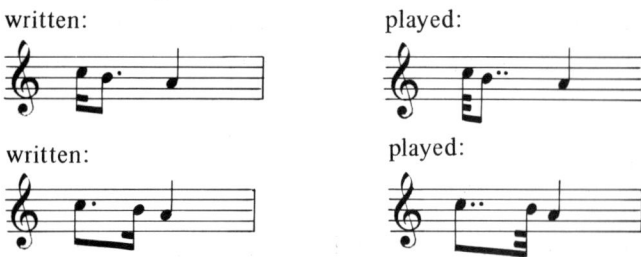

Evidence of the prolongation of the dot is found in the *Clavier-Büchlein* in *Invention No. 9*, in which the turn in measure 16 is written out in full:

The practice of lengthening the value of the dot is especially important in the cadential formula ♩.♪|♩, which may often be played ♩..♪|♩. (A trill may be added on the first note, as mentioned under *EXTEMPORIZATION OF ORNAMENTS*.)

The final cadence of *Invention No. 2* will serve as an example of the lengthening of the dot in the cadence.

The exaggeration of the dot is used by some artists in *Sinfonia No. 5:*

After using the term "always" in his discussion of the practice of lengthening the dot, C. P. E. Bach adds, "there are exceptions, and one should examine the melodic lines carefully."

Other examples of inexact notation of time values will be mentioned in footnotes when they occur.

PHRASING AND ARTICULATION

It was with reluctance that the editor of this volume decided to indicate suggested phrasing, even in print lighter than the rest of the text. In the *Autograph of 1723* only *Inventions No. 3, 9* and *15* and *Sinfonia No. 9* contain any slurs. The *Clavier-Büchlein* has none at all.

Bach's original slurs are probably intended to simply indicate a legato style of playing. Not one of these slurs crosses a bar line. This implies that they should be treated as if they were bowing indications for stringed instruments, as they are used when a legato performance is desired, with no noticeable separations or lifts between slurs. In other words, the present editor does not consider these slurs to be indications of articulation. The final decision about the interpretation of these slurs must rest with the performer.

Emanuel Winternitz, in Volume I of his *MUSICAL AUTOGRAPHS*, published by Dover Press, suggests that the directions of the stems of notes in some early manuscripts, including those of J. S. Bach, may be helpful in determining the articulation desired by the composer. This seems plausible and may apply in some measures of the 1723 autograph of the *Inventions* and *Sinfonias*. We will cite two examples.

The stems of *Invention No. 1* coincide with the general concept of its phrasing:

The stems in *Invention No. 15* might indicate detached notes on the second and fourth counts of the first measure and the second count of the second measure:

Because Bach often wrote large intervals in this fashion, it is doubtful that the change of direction of note stems within the same count always indicated some sort of articulation, but examples like the two shown above occur frequently and are too remarkable to ignore. For this reason, such situations have been duly taken into account in determining the phrasing recommended in this edition.

We have made it very clear that the phrasing indications in light print in this edition are to be regarded only as editorial suggestions. Teachers and students who are conversant with baroque music and are familiar with the performance practices of that era, and who have listened to this music played by fine artists, should feel free to form their own opinions. Indeed, we encourage them to analyze the subject matter of the music, the basic patterns and configurations, etc., determining for themselves the logic of grouping certain notes together and separating others. Subjects to be used in canonic imitation should, of course, be played with similar phrasing at each occurrence. Subject and countersubject, on the other hand, should usually have contrasting articulation. Students who make their own analysis will certainly profit from such a study and will play the selections more convincingly as a result, even if they disagree completely with our editorial suggestions.

DYNAMICS

Bach gave no indications of dynamics in any of the *Inventions* and *Sinfonias*. We have added editorial suggestions in lighter print. Our remarks under the subject of *PHRASING AND ARTICULATION* will apply also to dynamics. Students are encouraged to think for themselves.

If these works are to be played as they might have sounded on the clavichord, the dynamics range should be between *ppp* and *mf*. If they are to be played as they might have sounded on the harpsichord, the sound can be made somewhat louder, but crescendo and diminuendo are practically eliminated. Scholars have argued that they were solely for the clavichord, and others that they were solely for the harpsichord. More have been convinced that Bach intended them for all keyboard instruments.

It is certainly desirable that the student be aware of the characteristics and limitations of the instruments for which this music may have been written, but it seems foolish to limit the resources of the piano to correspond to the weaknesses of these instruments, when we cannot at the same time expand its possibilities to embrace the few advantages offered by them.

Contrapuntal music on the keyboard does not demand tremendous differences in dynamics. The effect is rather that of a conversation—each voice adding its opinion with sufficient volume and contrast to be audible, but not so much as to completely overshadow the others. An occasional whisper is effective, but to have every voice shouting at once would obscure the contribution of each voice and thus, generally speaking, double fortes are not idiomatic to this type of music.

We would discourage an expressionless, abstract interpretation of this music and at the same time condemn an overly romanticized version, with sweeping crescendos and melodramatic contrasts.

Teachers and students are warned against slavishly following the editorial suggestions for dynamics. The artistic performer must have a part in the creation of the music he produces. Consider the fact that the first dynamic indication for *Invention No. 1* is *f* in the *Busoni* edition, *mf* in the *Mason* edition and *p* in the *Czerny* edition. Who can say that any of these is wrong? A great deal depends on the way each of these beginnings is developed and completed.

Rather than add another opinion to the existing surplus, we have generally adopted dynamic indications similar to those of Hans Bischoff.

PEDALING

Use of the sustaining pedal is best avoided in the performance of the *Inventions* and *Sinfonias*. This is not merely because the keyboard instruments of Bach's day were not equipped with sustaining pedals. Unless the sustaining pedal is used with extreme care, it tends to obscure contrapuntal lines. It is difficult to keep the pedal from sounding anachronistic in this type of music. Rather than take this chance, it is best for the student to leave pedaling out of this music completely. It would be wrong to say that it cannot ever be used in good taste, to ensure a legato at certain points. But the compositions were constructed to be played without a sustaining pedal, and for this very reason most of the longer leaps occur at points where the legato phrase SHOULD be broken. Many of the greatest artists play all of these works without ever touching the sustaining pedal.

The una corda ("soft") pedal may be used judiciously for dynamic contrasts, but the pianist should avoid relying on it to the extent that he uses it in every soft passage. It is most effective in terraced dynamics or echo effects.

TEMPO

Bach left no tempo indications for any of the *Inventions* and *Sinfonias*. The table below was compiled from early editions, from scholarly commentaries, and from the recorded performances of various artists.

Several of the recorded artists play with a considerable amount of rubato, and with fluctuations of tempo, sometimes almost from measure to measure. Erwin Bodky* chose to relate all of his tempo indications to the human pulse-beat, and to round out his indications to end with zeros. To these he added "plus-or-minus" signs, as might well be appropriate for all of the indications in the following table.

The widespread divergence of supposedly knowledgeable opinion could be the subject of a long discussion. In *Invention No. 1*, compare Czerny's and Andras Schiff's ♩ = 120 with Glenn Gould's ♩ = 60.

The present editor would be the last to say that any of the tempos in this table are wrong. We believe that this table will show that almost any reasonable tempo works well enough in the hands of an artist who has convictions about the chosen tempo. And this may be the lesson to be learned; experienced students or artists need not be bound by editorial tempo suggestions (or any other editorial indications, for that matter) with which they strongly disagree.

It is also well to remember that tempos may vary with factors other than the taste or moods of the individual, including the responsiveness and tonal clarity of a particular instrument, as well as the acoustics and resonance of a room or hall.

It was completely in the baroque spirit to leave the choice of tempo to the performer.

			EDITIONS		COMMENTARIES				RECORDINGS						
	M.M.	Bischoff	Czerny	Bodky*	Keller**	Martin Galling	Kenneth Gilbert	Glenn Gould	Christiane Jaccottet	Ralph Kirkpatrick	Ton Koopman	Wanda Landowska	George Malcolm	Andras Schiff
INVENTION 1	♩	96	120	±80	63	66	63	60	80	76+	72	63	76	120
INVENTION 2	♩	69	108	±80	52	63	63	40	72	60+	60	60+	80	112
INVENTION 3	♩.	60	80	±60	46	48	48+	66	58	52	46	42	52	52
INVENTION 4	♩.	76	72	±60	60	60	60	72	52	64	58	58	84	76
INVENTION 5	♩	72	108	±80	72	63	84	100+	88	76	72	104	100	96
INVENTION 6	♪	138	144	±120	96	104	104	92	120	80	120	88+	112	112
INVENTION 7	♩	69	112	±60	72	66	63+	108+	76	52	58	48	84	56
INVENTION 8	♩	126	144	±100	116–126	120	112	100	112	120	116	112	120	120
INVENTION 9	♩	60	116	±60	46	50	63	40	48	60	60	58	80	63
INVENTION 10	♩.	100	152	±100	108	104	96	160	120	96	108	96+	120	96
INVENTION 11	♩	80	108	±80	58	60	84	112	44	100	72	88	72+	96
INVENTION 12	♩.	76	84	±60	72	69	50	100	60	69+	48	69+	69+	76
INVENTION 13	♩	116	104	±80	69	66	88	144+	92	104	84	104	112	84
INVENTION 14	♩	69	88	±60	88	56	54	52	66	40	66	56	66	63
INVENTION 15	♩	96	104	±80	92	96	54	104	76	80	84	63	84	80

*Bodky, Erwin. See *RECOMMENDED READING*, on the following page.
**Keller, Hermann. *Die Klavierwerke Bachs*, Edition Peters, Leipzig, 1950.

Recordings Used

Galling, Martin, *HARPSICHORD*. Vox Archive ACD 8028.

Gilbert, Kenneth, *HARPSICHORD*. Digital Stereo 415 112-2 Archiv Production.

Gould, Glenn, *PIANO*. Columbia MS56622.

Jaccottet, Christiane, *HARPSICHORD*. Pilz CD 160 134.

Kirkpatrick, Ralph, *HARPSICHORD*. ARC 73174, Archiv.

Koopman, Ton, *HARPSICHORD*. Capriccio Digital Stereo 10 210.

Landowska, Wanda, *HARPSICHORD*. Memorial Edition, RCA Victor LM 2389.

Malcolm, George, *HARPSICHORD*. Nonesuch H71144.

Schiff, Andras, *PIANO*. Decca 411 974-2 London.

Recommended Reading

Bach, Carl Philipp Emanuel. *Versuch über die wahre Art das Clavier zu spielen*. Berlin, 1753; English translation, W. J. Mitchell, *Essay on the True Art of Playing Keyboard Instruments*. W. W. Norton & Co., New York, 1949.

Bodky, Erwin. *The Interpretation of Bach's Keyboard Music*. Harvard University Press, Cambridge, Massachusetts, 1960.

Couperin, François. *L'art de toucher le clavecin*. Paris, 1716, enl. ed. Paris, 1717; English translation, Margery Halford, Alfred Publishing Co., Van Nuys, California, 1974.

Dart, Thurston. *The Interpretation of Music*. Harper and Row, New York, 1963.

David, Hans T. & Mendel, Arthur. *The Bach Reader, A Life of Johann Sebastian Bach in Letters and Documents*. W. W. Norton & Co., New York, 1945. Revised ed., 1966.

Dolmetsch, Arnold. *The Interpretation of the Music of the XVII and XVIII Centuries*. Novello & Co., London, 1946.

Donington, Robert. *The Interpretation of Early Music, New Version*. St. Martin's Press, New York, 1973.

Dorian, Frederick. *The History of Music in Performance*. W. W. Norton & Co., New York, 1942.

Emery, Walter. *Bach's Ornaments*. Novello & Co., London, 1953.

Ferguson, Howard. *Keyboard Interpretation from the 14th to the 19th Century*. Oxford University Press, New York & London, 1965.

Jorgensen, Owen. *Tuning the Historical Temperaments by Ear*. Northern Michigan University Press, Marquette, 1977.

Jorgensen, Owen. *TUNING/Containing/The Perfection of Eighteenth Century Temperament/The Lost Art of Nineteenth Century Temperament/and/The Science of Equal Temperament*. Michigan State University Press, East Lansing, 1991.

Neumann, Frederick. *Ornamentation in Baroque and Post-Baroque Music*. Princeton University Press, Princeton, New Jersey, 1978.

Palmer, Willard A., & Halford, Margery. *The Baroque Era, an Introduction to the Keyboard Music*. Alfred Publishing Co., Inc., Van Nuys, California, 1976.

Quantz, Johann Joachim, *Versuch einer Anweisung, die Flöte traversiere zu spielen*. Berlin, 1752; English translation by Edward R. O'Reilly, *On Playing the Flute*. Faber & Faber, London, 1966.

Restout, Denise. *Landowska on Music*. Stein and Day, New York, 1964.

Türk, Daniel Gottlieb. *Klavierschule*. Leipzig & Halle, 1789; English translation by Raymond H. Haggh, *School of Clavier Playing*. University of Nebraska Press, Lincoln & London, 1982.

Acknowledgments

I would like to express my thanks to Judith Schneider for her valuable assistance in the preparation of the manuscript of the first Masterwork edition of the *Inventions* and *Sinfonias*, and for her help with the research necessary for its completion. I also wish to thank Owen Jorgensen for helpful suggestions in the preparation of the foreword of the present edition. Thanks are also due to Lynlee Alley for her assistance in tabulating the metronome tempos. Sharon Aaronson is due thanks for her help in bringing this newly revised edition to completion. Most of all, I wish to thank Morton and Iris Manus, the guiding spirits of Alfred Publishing Company, whose unfailing support and encouragement have made all of my Masterwork editions and other educational materials possible, and whose high standards should be an inspiration to all music editors and publishers.

And to my dear wife, Ruby Touchstone Palmer, my treasure now for 50 years, who continues to make my work as pleasant and free of care as possible, no amount of thanks can ever suffice.

Invention No. 1
in C Major

BWV 772

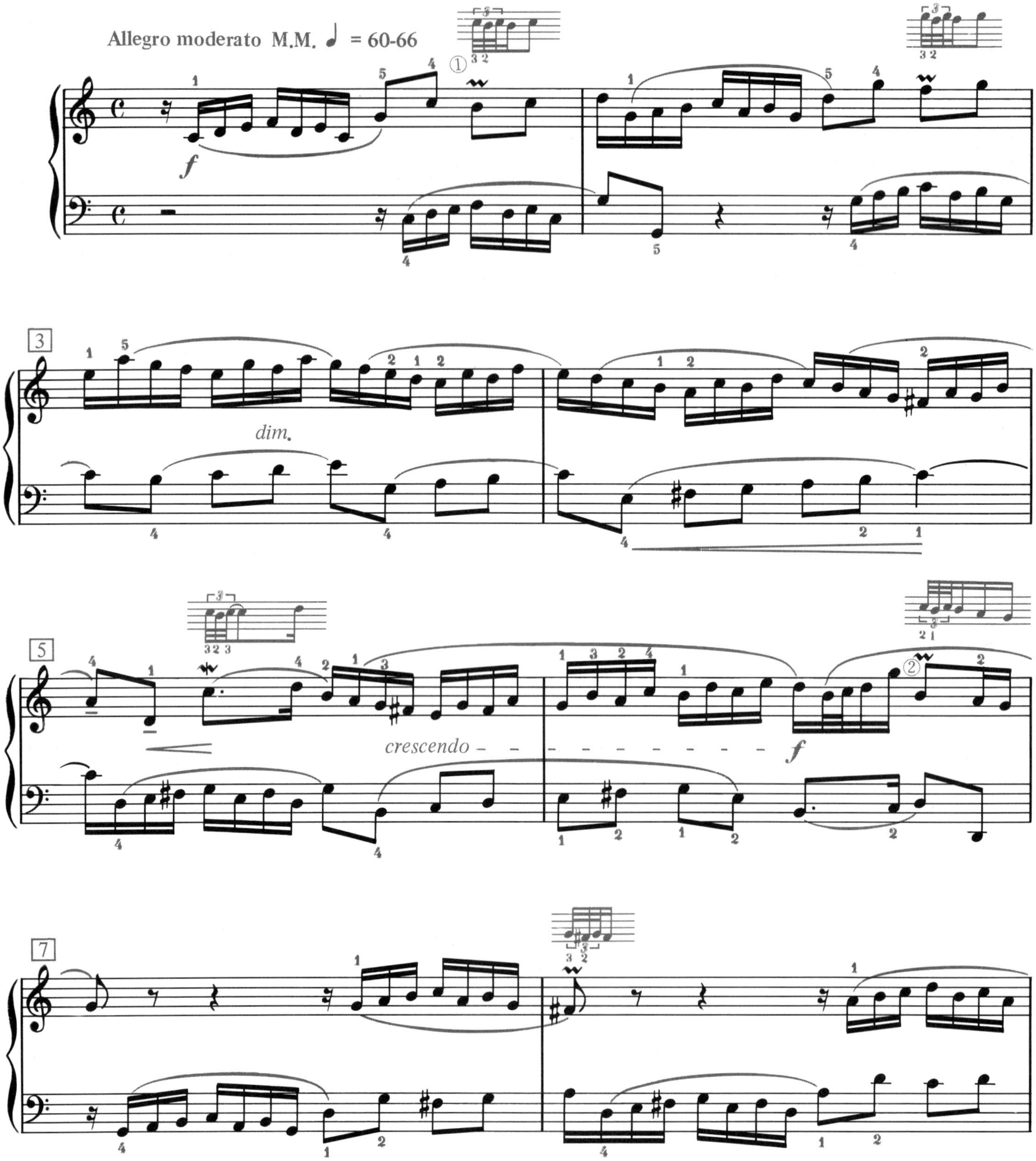

Allegro moderato M.M. ♩ = 60-66

① ALL manuscripts show a TRILL here. The mordent on this note, which appears in the *Busoni* edition, the *Czerny* edition and the *Mason* edition, is without foundation.

This trill and the trill in the following measure might also be played as pralltrillers (see discussion on page 11) or as trills with termination (see page 6).

② The trill at the cadence may be played with additional repercussions:

③④ These trills in parentheses appear in the *Clavier-Büchlein*. They should be included. Trills at such cadences are part of the tradition of the Baroque period. They may be played with more repercussions:

⑤ The bass line in the *Clavier-Büchlein* ends as follows:

⑥ The arpeggio sign appears in the final autograph. It is played the same as in modern notation.

Invention No. 1
in C Major

BWV 772a

VARIANT CONTAINED IN THE *AUTOGRAPH OF 1723*

This version of *Invention No. 1* appears in the *Friedemann manuscript* of 1723. The added notes seem to have been written into the manuscript later. They might have been added by J. S. Bach himself, to show that it was permissible to vary even the subject matter of a composition by adding passing tones. The triplets were clearly indicated.

It was not the practice during this period, however, to combine binary and ternary rhythms. Wherever triplets were written against two notes it was customary to alter the ternary rhythms to fit the binary ones, or vice versa, depending on the prevailing rhythm of the composition. If the groups of four 16ths are accommodated to the triplet rhythm, the first and third notes (or rests) in the group must be lengthened and the second and fourth shortened. The triplets may be accommodated to the 16ths by playing each triplet as two 16th notes followed by an eighth note.

Glenn Gould, in his recording of the *Two and Three Part Inventions* (Columbia MS 6622), has chosen to use some of these added notes and to omit others. He uses the following rhythm:

Invention No. 2
in C Minor

BWV 773

If a slow tempo is chosen, all trills may be played with additional repercussions. In such a case it is probably best to preserve the legato style throughout.

①②③④ Some editors believe that these ornaments and the corresponding ones later in the composition should be interpreted as examples of the "Schneller" or "Imperfect Shake." See the discussion on page 11.

If such is the case, they are played: 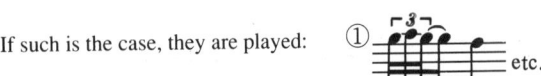 etc.

This conclusion is due to the fact that consecutive octaves result if the trill in measure 3 is begun on the upper auxiliary. C. P. E. Bach, however, states in his *ESSAY* that the Schneller is always written out in full. This may be reason enough to conclude that the use of the Schneller in any of the *Inventions* is incorrect.

⑤ This trill does not appear in any autograph. It is added in the *Bach-Gesellschaft* edition. Apart from its usual function in the cadence, the ornament is logical because of the canonic structure of this invention. Since the trill is used in the left hand at the end of the eighth measure, the canon is clarified by playing the trill in the right hand in the sixth measure.

⑥ The tie does not appear in the *Clavier-Büchlein*.

⑦ Consecutive unisons result from beginning the trill on the upper note, but the performance of the ornament as a Schneller does not solve the problem (if indeed there is a problem other than the fact that the composition was written to be played on an instrument with two manuals). The realization shown here is possible. The Schneller is impossible to perform in this measure.

⑧ More consecutive octaves result from starting the trill on the upper auxiliary.

⑨ See comment on this final cadence in the discussion of dotted rhythms beginning on page 13.

Invention No. 3
in D Major

Allegretto M.M. ♩. = 52-60

BWV 774

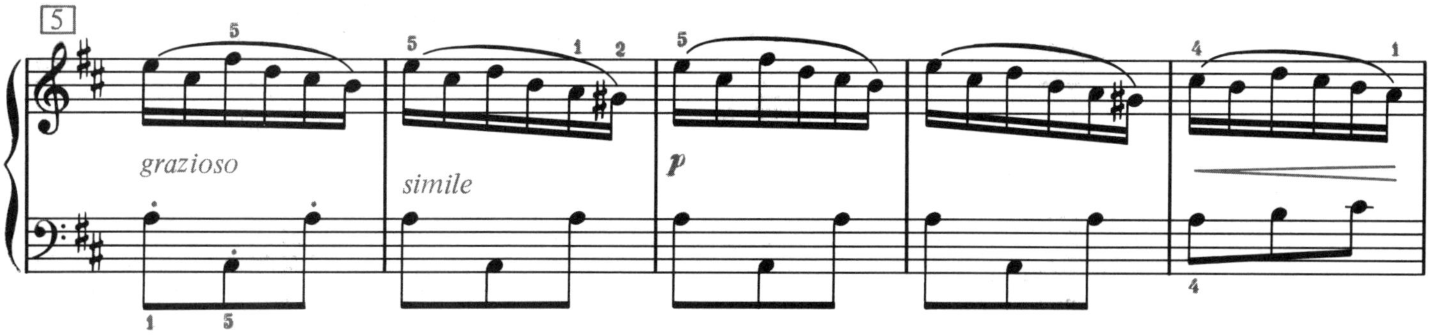

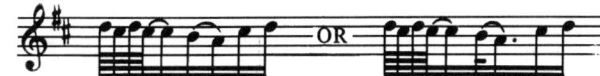

The slurs in dark print appear in the *Friedemann manuscript* in a manner that makes it impossible to know exactly which notes they encompass. Bach probably intended simply a legato style of playing.

The ornaments in the third and fourth measures (and those in the 45th and 46th measures) of this invention are highly controversial. They are clarified considerably by the *Clavier-Büchlein*. The trills in parentheses are from the *Clavier-Büchlein*.

① See the discussion of this ornament under *THE IMPORTANCE OF THE CLAVIER-BÜCHLEIN*, beginning on page 3.

② This ornament is discussed under *THE APPOGGIATURA USED AS A PASSING TONE*, beginning on page 10. After reading this discussion you may agree with the interpretation shown in the text. Nevertheless, here are other possibilities:

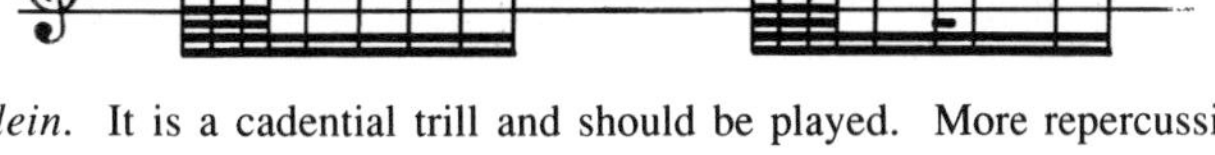

③ This trill appears only in the *Clavier-Büchlein*. It is a cadential trill and should be played. More repercussions may be used, and the dot may be lengthened:

④ This trill may be played with additional repercussions and with the value of the dot lengthened, in the same manner as ③ on the previous page.

Trills in lighter print on this and the following page are cadential trills, not indicated in either manuscript. They may be played with additional repercussions. See ③ on the previous page.

⑤ These notes are from the *Clavier-Büchlein*.

Invention No. 4
in D Minor

BWV 775

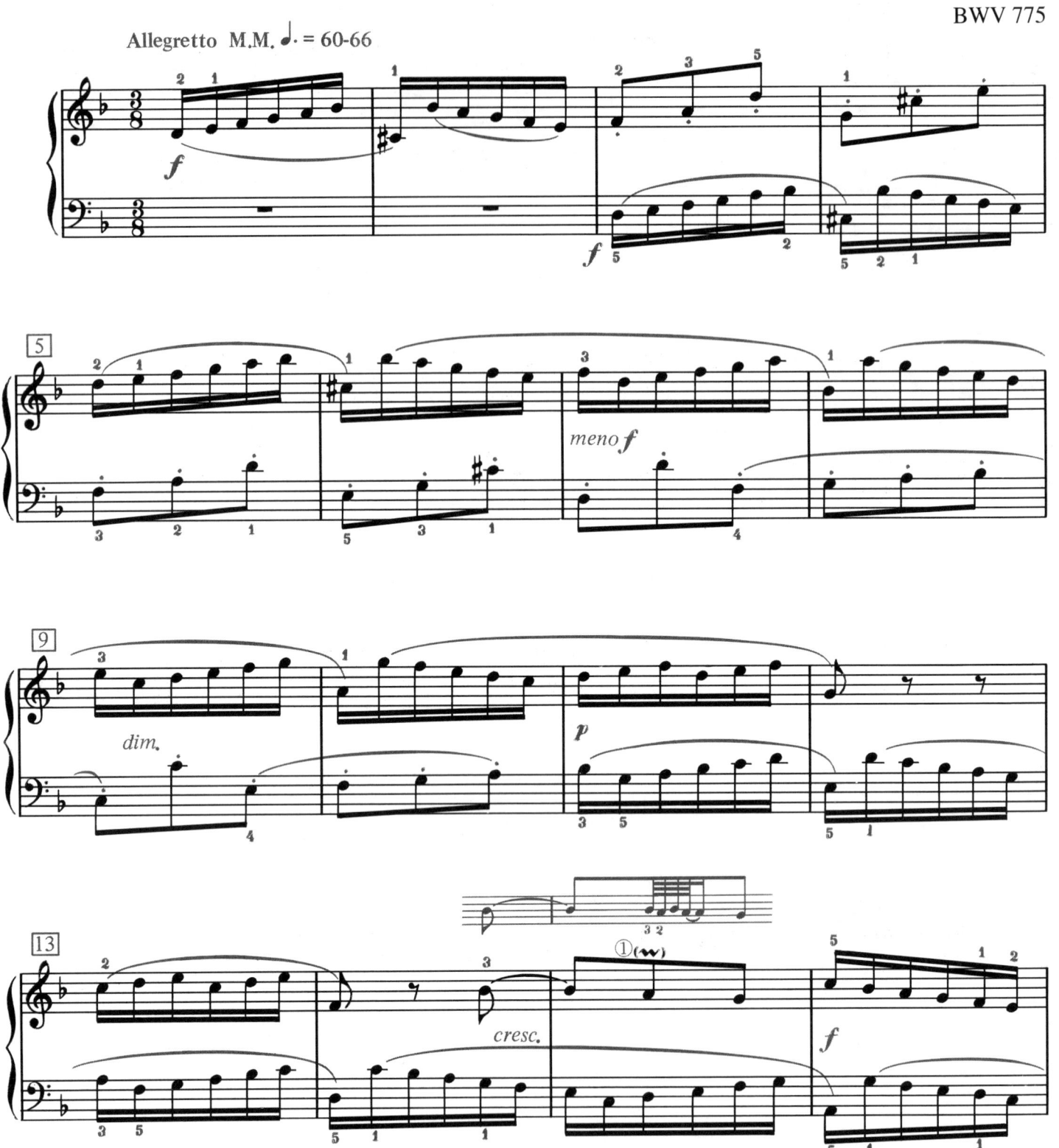

Traditionally, the 16th notes are played legato, and the eighth notes are played detached or staccato. The phrasing recommended here is suggested by the directions of note-stems in the *Autograph of 1723*.

① This ornament appears only in the *Clavier-Büchlein*. At a rapid tempo, the first note of the trill may be tied to the note preceding it. With this form of execution the ornament becomes a "Pralltriller":

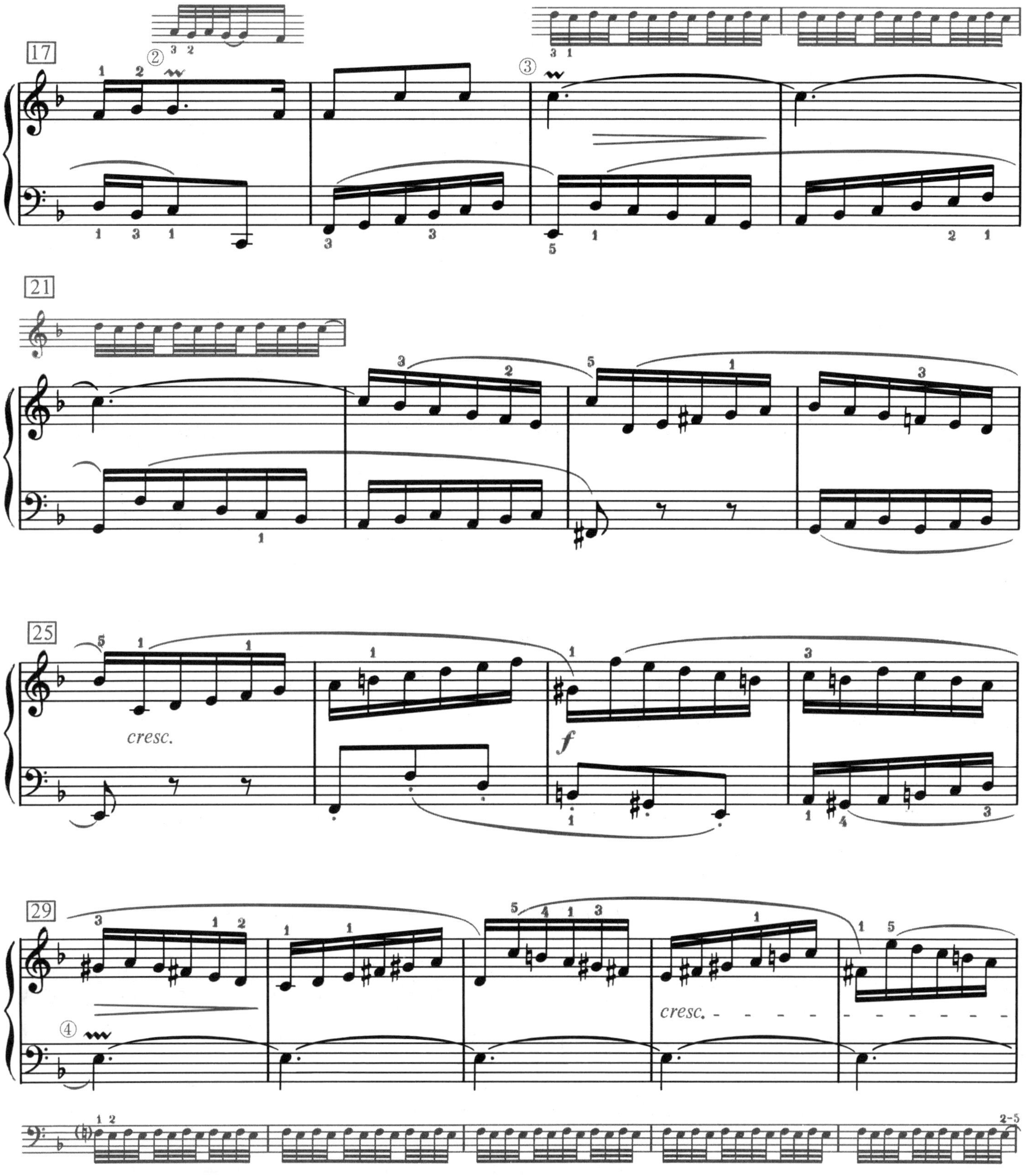

① This and other trills in lighter print are cadential trills, not found in the manuscripts. They may be played with additional repercussions, and the dot may be lengthened:

③④ The symbols tr, ᮣ and ᮣᮣ are used interchangeably by Bach. They all mean "Trillo" (trill). These long trills are the only means by which the tone may be sustained audibly for so many measures. The trills may be played with twice as many repercussions as shown, if desired.

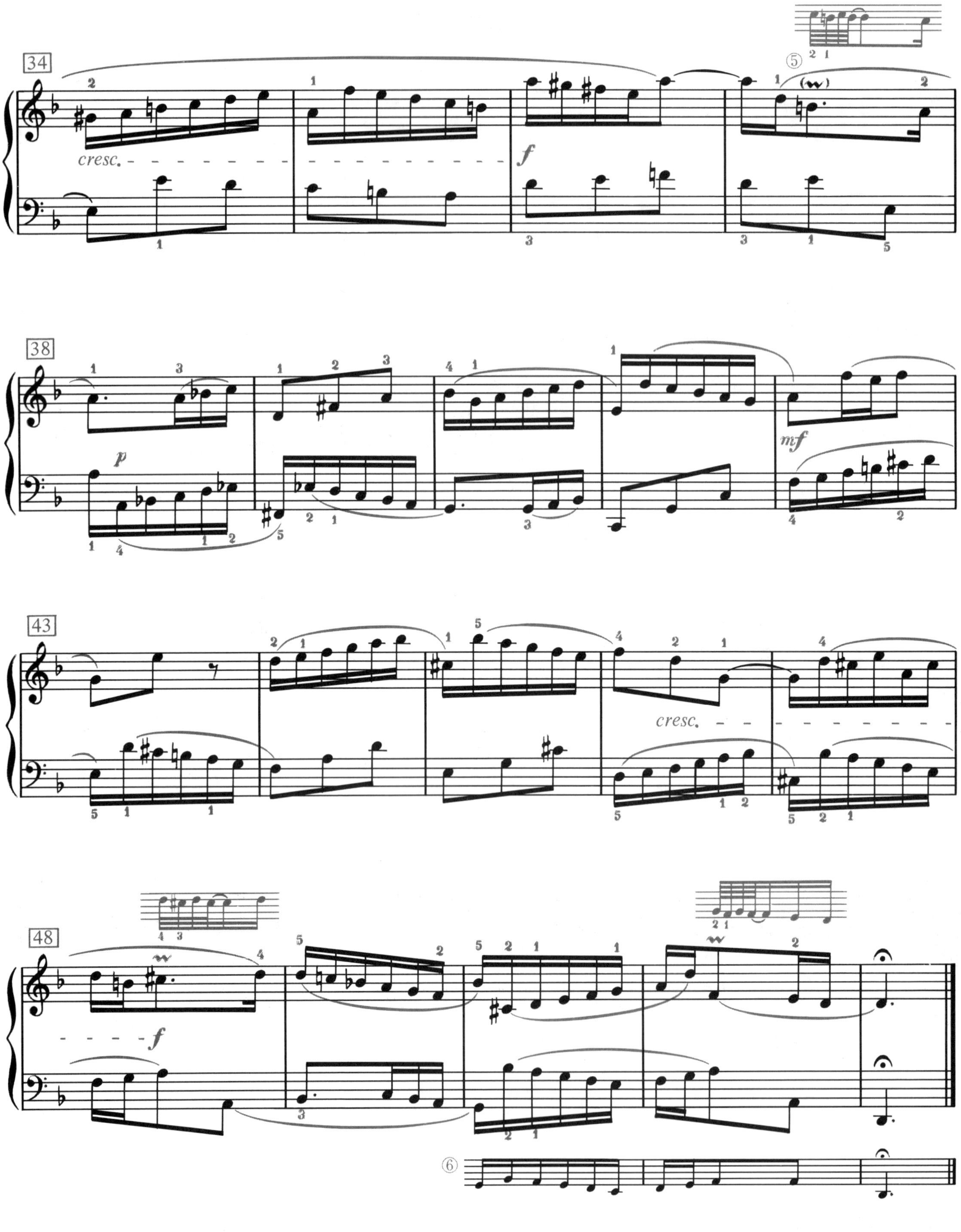

⑤ This trill is from the *Clavier-Büchlein*. It may be played with additional repercussions, and with the value of the dot lengthened:

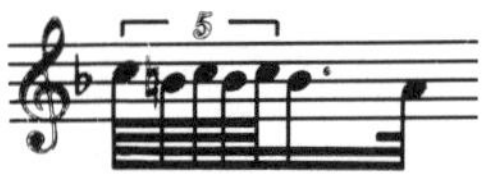

⑥ The lower staff is from the *Clavier-Büchlein*.

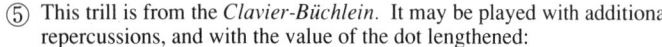

Invention No. 5
in E-flat Major

BWV 776

Allegro moderato M.M. ♩ = 100-108

①② The first mordent in the motive is often omitted. When the left hand plays the same theme in the fifth and sixth measures, corresponding ornaments are absent in all of the autographs. It would seem that a decision should be made as to whether the mordent be omitted or included throughout the work (see *THE EXTEMPORIZATION OF ORNAMENTS* on page 13). The ornaments are clearly indicated in the *Autograph of 1723*. Wanda Landowska played the mordents in the first eight measures exactly as shown in the text. After this she added and omitted ornaments according to her own fancy.

③ At a fast tempo this and all corresponding trills might be played as 32nd notes: or as pralltrillers:

④ This is an example of inexact notation, which was common during the Baroque period. See the discussion of this ornament on page 9.

⑤ In the *Clavier-Büchlein* a trill appears instead of this ornament. This is the only embellishment contained in this invention in the *Clavier-Büchlein*.

Invention No. 6
in E Major

BWV 777

This invention may be played legato throughout. The mordentlike figures, such as the ones in the right hand in the fourth measure, are brought out more effectively if the accompanying notes are played detached.

①② Small notes are from the *Clavier-Büchlein*.

Invention No. 7
in E Minor

BWV 778

①②③④⑤⑥ appear only in the *Clavier-Büchlein*.

⑦ The number of repercussions in the long trill depends on the tempo, but see footnote ⑨ on the following page.

⑧ The long trill may be ended with the suffix:

⑨ This trill appears only in the *Clavier-Büchlein*. It is necessary if the note is to be sustained, and there is no doubt that it should be played. Because of the short trill in the right hand, which is played with the starting notes of the left-hand trill, a minimum number of repercussions for the long trill is the number shown in this text.

⑩ The *Bach-Gesellschaft* has d♯², which does not appear in either autograph, although it does appear in the bass in measure 18.

⑪ From this point the *Clavier-Büchlein* has the following:

Invention No. 8

in F Major

BWV 779

Vivace M.M. ♩ = 112-120

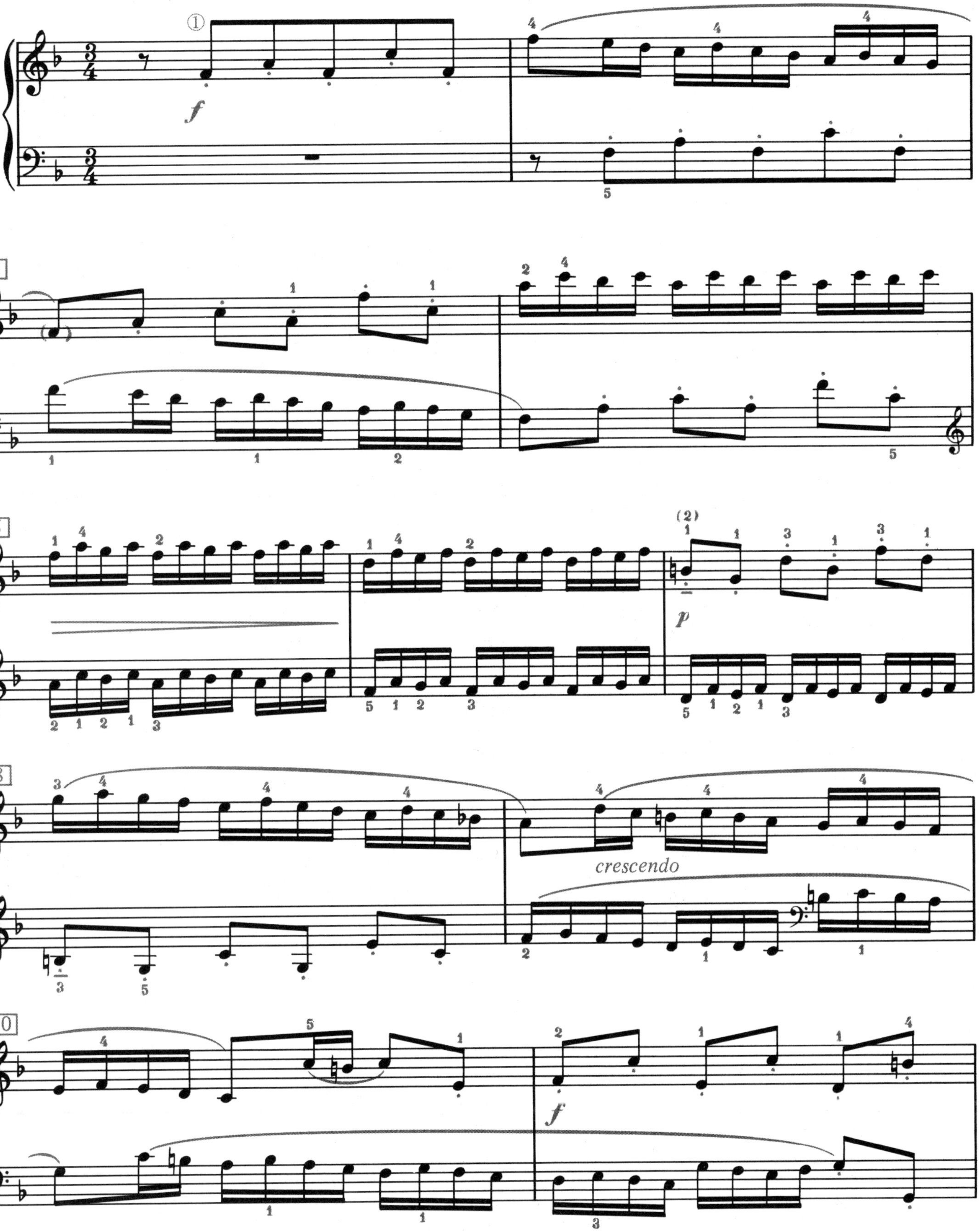

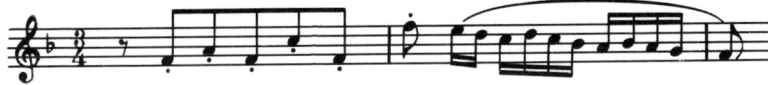

① *Busoni* phrases as follows, but is inconsistent (in several measures he uses the phrasing suggested in this edition).

② The *Clavier-Büchlein* omits measures 17, 18, 19 and 20.

③ The notes on the smaller staff are those found in the *Clavier-Büchlein* as the bass line of measures 21, 22 and 23.

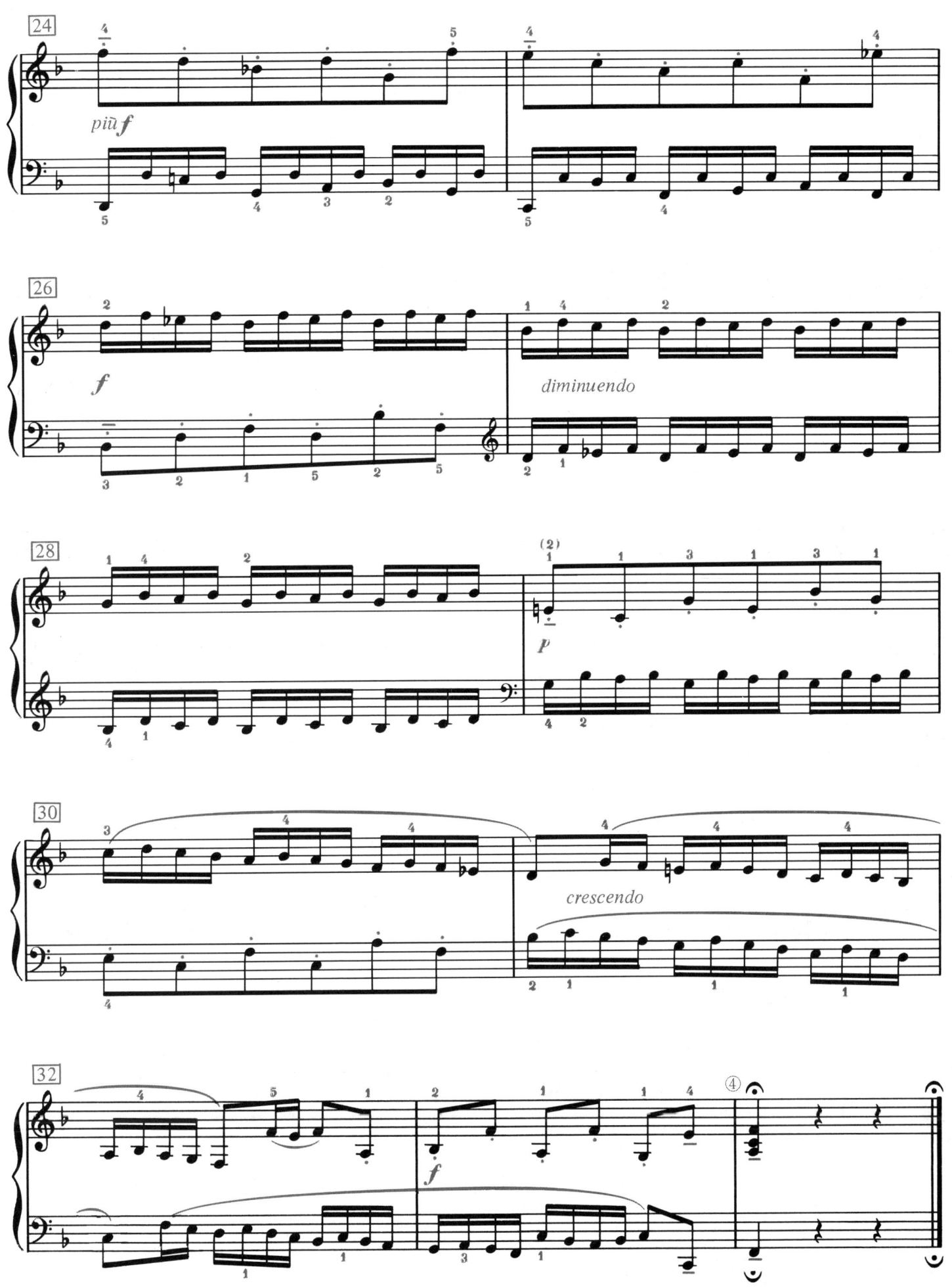

④ The *Clavier-Büchlein* shows the fermata over the last chord.

Invention No. 9
in F Minor

BWV 780

Andante con espressione M.M. ♩ = 52-60

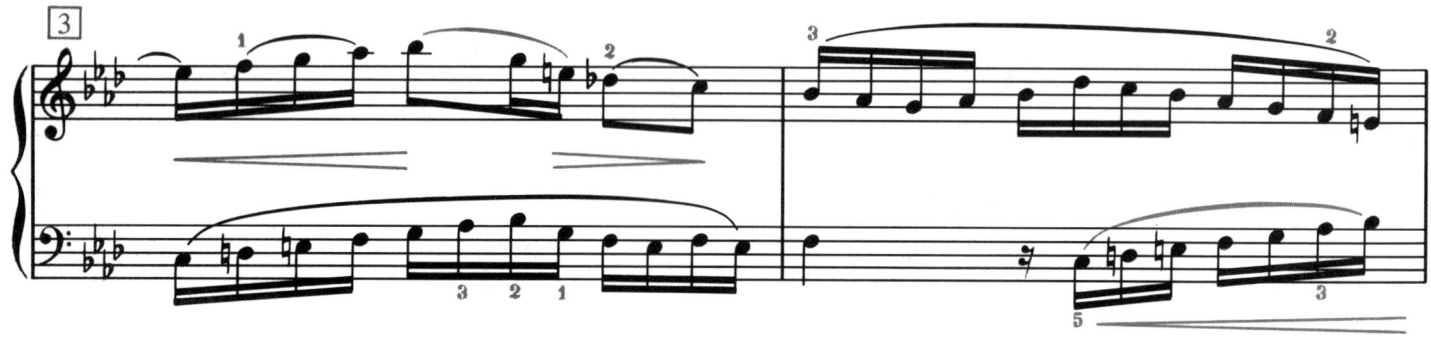

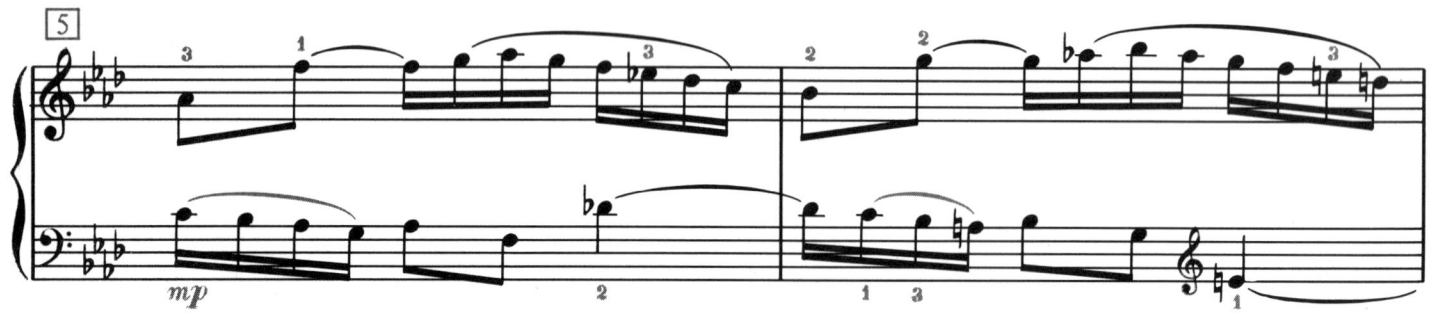

The slurs in dark print, from the *Autograph of 1723*, are missing in the *Clavier-Büchlein*. These slurs indicate a legato, cantabile style throughout the piece, except for the short, disjunct motives, which should be lightly detached. An abrupt lift at the end of each slur is not intended. The slurs in light print are derived from those that occur in similar passages in the final autograph.

① The *Clavier-Büchlein* has e♭².

② The *Autograph of 1723* has an a♮. The ♮ sign does not appear in the *Clavier-Büchlein*.

③ The *Autograph of 1723* has d♭. The *Clavier-Büchlein* has d♮.

④ The *Bach-Gesellschaft* shows . The *Autograph of 1723* has . (The *Clavier-Büchlein* has no ornaments in this invention.)

⑤ The *Bach-Gesellschaft* shows , a trill with termination. *Bischoff* has the double mordent.

⑥ The *Clavier-Büchlein* shows the turn written out in full:

⑦ See discussion under 5 (*THE TRILL WITH PREFIX FROM BELOW*) on page 7. Also see *DOTTED RHYTHMS IN THE BAROQUE PERIOD*, beginning on page 13.

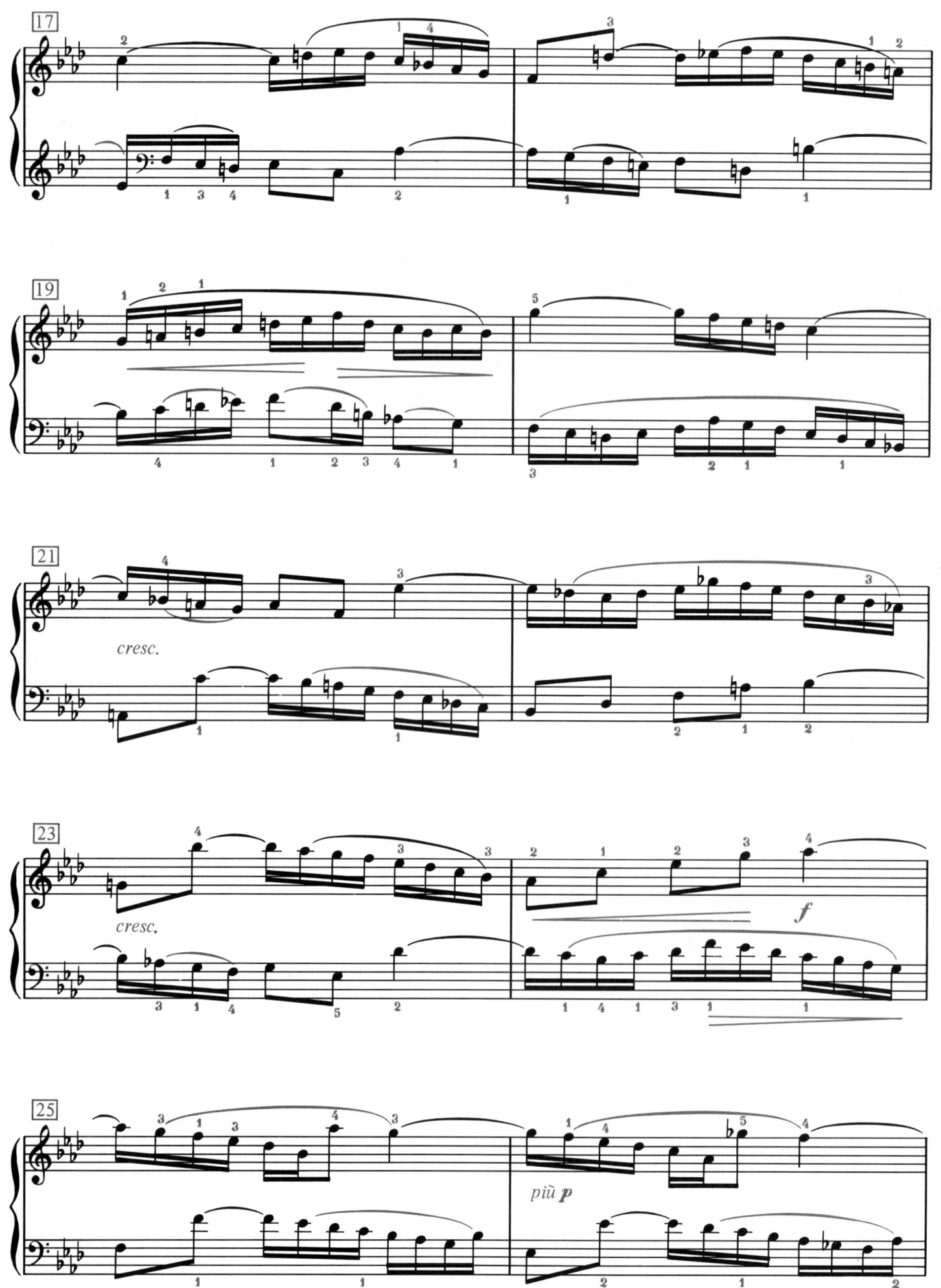

⑧ The value of the dot may be increased:
See discussion under 6 (*THE TRILL
WITH PREFIX FROM ABOVE*) on page 7.

In the *Autograph of 1723*, this ornament could possibly be ⋏⋏ , in which case it is played:
See 13 (*THE PREPARED TRILL*) on page 10.

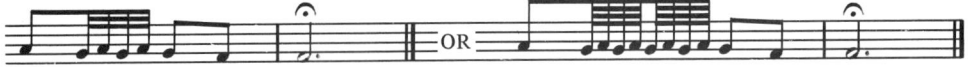

Invention No. 10
in G Major

BWV 781

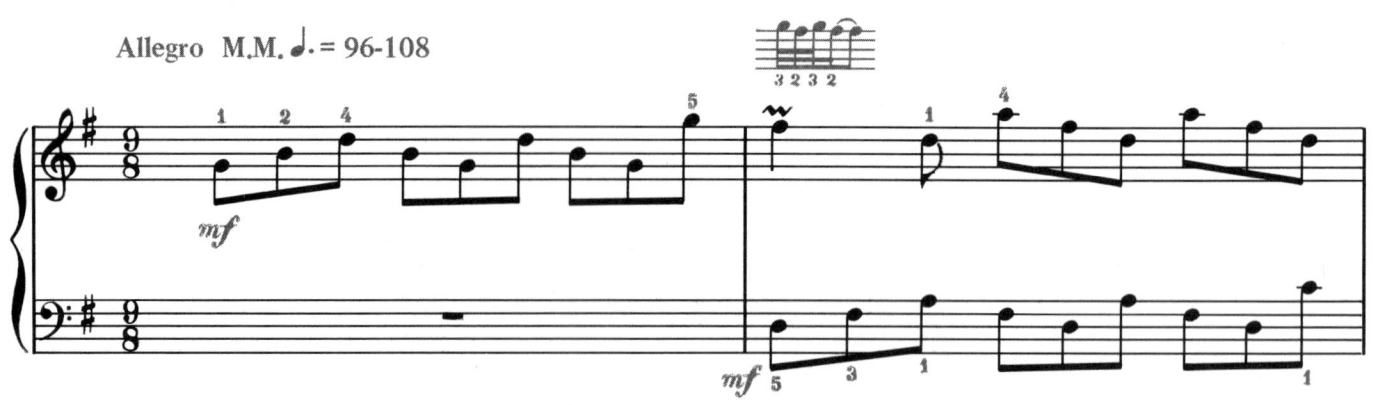

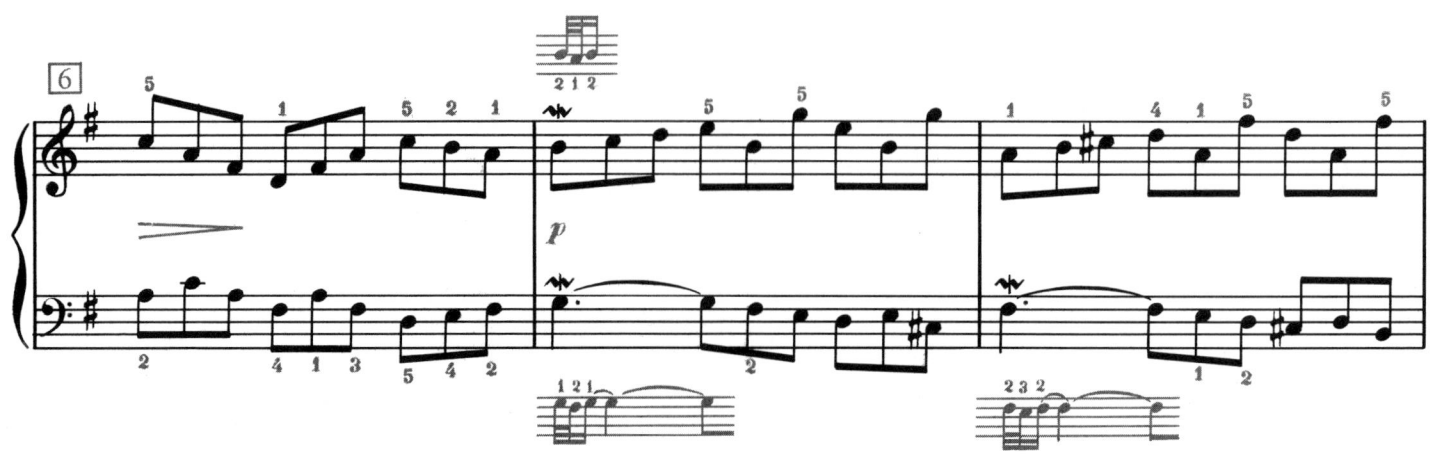

This invention is traditionally played detached throughout. *Busoni* has *sempre staccato*. *Bischoff, Mason* and *Czerny* indicate no phrasing.

Invention No. 11
in G Minor

BWV 782

① This invention is often performed at a faster tempo. A slower tempo is suggested by the ornaments in measure 10, which are usually omitted. The 16th notes are usually played legato and the eighth notes detached, except as indicated. The mordents should be played as quickly as possible, regardless of the note values in the realizations.

② The *Clavier-Büchlein* has the d² x'd out and replaced with a b♭¹:

③ All of the trills in this invention are preceded by the upper note. They may be tied to the previous note and played as pralltrillers (see page 11).

④ See the discussion of *THE TRILL WITH PREFIX FROM BELOW, WITH TERMINATION*, on page 8.

⑤ The *Autograph of 1723* has A♮ here (no accidental indicated). The *Clavier-Büchlein* has A♭.

⑥ In the *Clavier-Büchlein* the last three measures are as follows:

Invention No. 12
in A Major

BWV 783

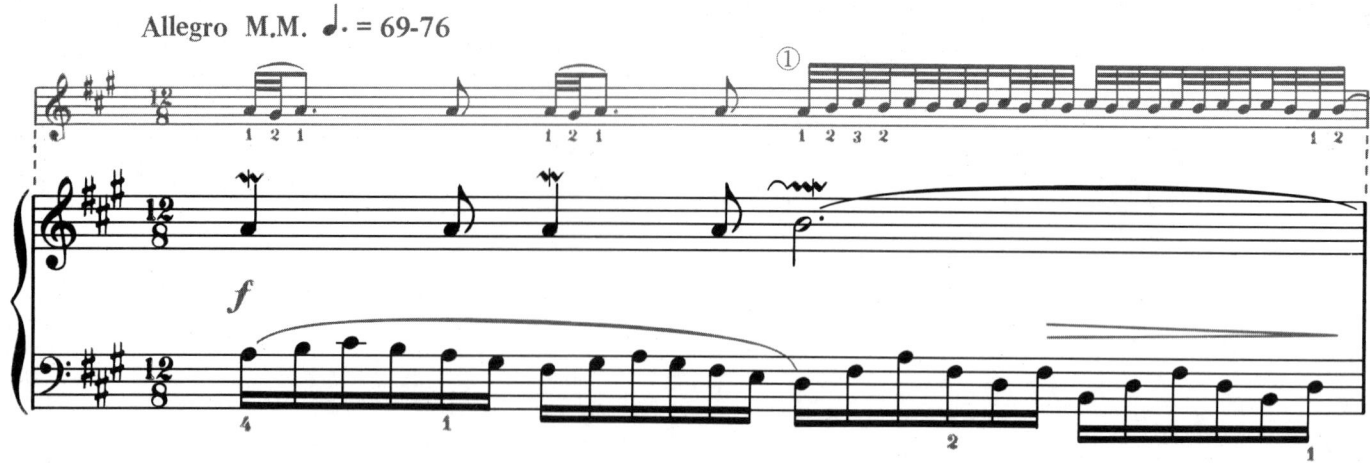

① This manner of execution of the trill with prefix from below, with termination, allows consistency throughout the selection, including the trill in the next to last measure, which is not tied. The use of the ornament in this invention is discussed on page 8.

② The *Clavier-Büchlein* has:

③ The *Clavier-Büchlein* has: etc.

④ The *Clavier-Büchlein* has c♯² instead of f♯².

⑤ A trill at the cadence is appropriate:

Invention No. 13
in A Minor

BWV 784

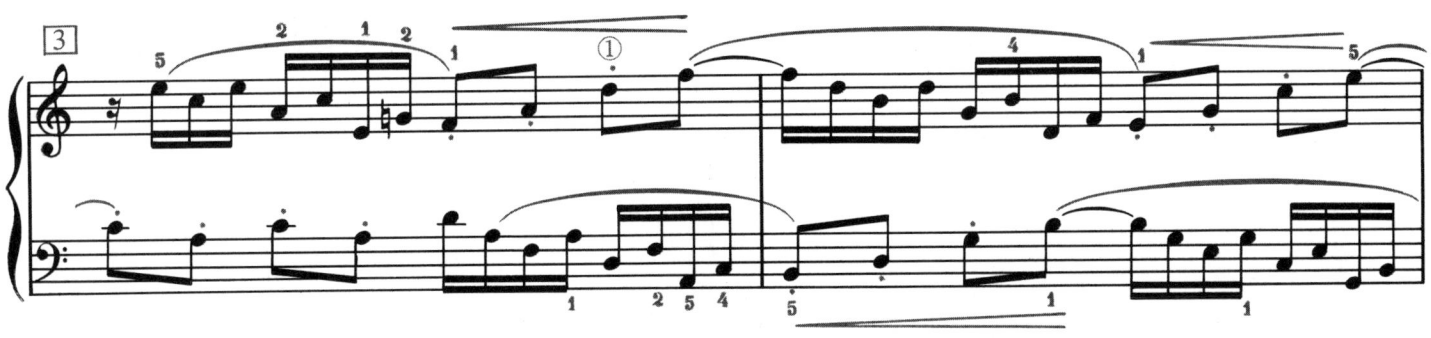

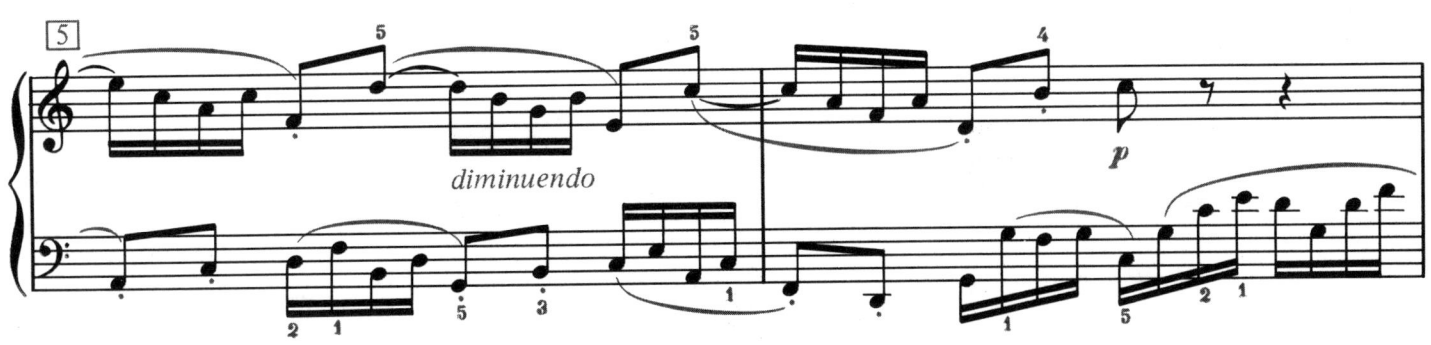

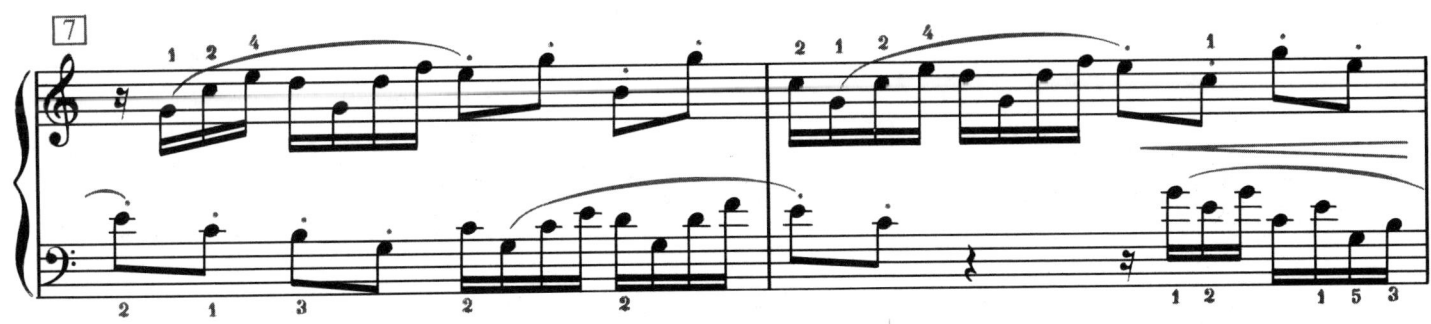

① The *Clavier-Büchlein* has c² instead of d².

② The treble d²'s and the bass d¹ in this count are ♯ in the *Clavier-Büchlein*.

③ Many editions have a♭². It is clearly a♮² in both autographs.

④ From this measure on, the *Clavier-Büchlein* ends as shown at the bottom of the next page.

From measure 16 on, the *Clavier-Büchlein* ends thus:

Invention No. 14
in B-flat Major

BWV 785

Andante con moto M.M. ♩ = 52-56

① The *Clavier-Büchlein* has d² instead of a¹.

The *Clavier-Büchlein* ends thus:

Invention No. 15
in B Minor

BWV 786

Allegro moderato M.M. ♩ = 80-88

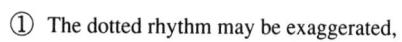
① The dotted rhythm may be exaggerated,  (see discussion beginning on page 13).

② This F♯ and the following G♯ are eighth notes in the *Clavier-Büchlein*.

leggieramente
staccato

③ In the *Clavier-Büchlein* the first a¹ in this group of 16th notes has no accidental; the second a¹ has a sharp.

④ The value of the dot may be exaggerated: